P9-AQT-070

EDWARD WESTON

HARRY CALLAHAN

PHOTOESPAÑA

This book was produced
in collaboration with PhotoEspaña

CHAIRMAN
Alberto Anaut

DIRECTOR
Claude Bussac

CENERAL CURATOR
Gerardo Mosquera

DEPUTY DIRECTOR
Luis Posada

EXHIBITION MANAGER
Emily Adams

EXHIBITION
CURATOR
Laura González Flores

CORDINATION
Emily Adams
Ana Berruguete

DESIGN
Joaquín Gallego / Laura González Flores

BOOK
COORDINATOR
Ana Belén García

GRAPHIC DESIGN
Estudio Joaquín Gallego
María Alén

PROOFREADING
Álvaro Villa

TRANSLATIONS
Art in Translation

REPRODUCTIONS
Cromotex

PRINTING
Brizzolis, arte en gráficas

LA FABRICA

PUBLISHER
Alberto Anaut

EDITORIAL DIRECTOR
Camino Brasa

DEVELOPMENT DIRECTOR
Fernando Paz

PRODUCTION DIRECTOR
Paloma Castellanos

ORGANISER
Rosa Ureta

La Fábrica
Verónica, 13
28014 Madrid
Tel + 34 91 360 13 20
Fax + 34 91 360 13 22
e-mail: edicion@lafabrica.com

The typeface used in this book is Celeste
And it has been printed on Tatami Symbol 150 gsm.
and Pop'Set 150 gsm

COVER ILLUSTRATION:
Edward Weston. *Nude*, 1936
Collection Center for Creative Photography, The University of Arizona
© 1981 Center for Creative Photography, Arizona Board of Regents

BACK COVER ILLUSTRATION:
Harry Callahan. *Eleanor*, 1948
Collection Center for Creative Photography, The University of Arizona
Courtesy Pace/MacGill Gallery, New York
© The Estate of Harry Callahan

© this edition: La Fábrica, 2013

© the texts: their authors
© images:

Edward Weston
Collection Center for Creative Photography, The University of Arizona
© 1981 Center for Creative Photography, Arizona Board of Regents

Harry Callahan
Collection Center for Creative Photography, The University of Arizona
Courtesy Pace/MacGill Gallery, Nueva York
© The Estate of Harry Callahan

ISBN: 978-84-15691-33-4
Legal Deposit: M-15708-2013

EDWARD WESTON

HARRY CALLAHAN

LA FABRICA EDITORIAL

FUNDACION
Banco Santander

1949 HARRY CALLAHAN

He, She, It

The Erotic Drive in the Photography of Edward Weston and Harry Callahan

Laura González Flores

She closes her eyes.

But isn't it he –Adam– who is supposed to fall asleep so that Eve can emerge from his side?

In the images that He constructs (in dreams?), it is She who surrenders to Hypnos. In Edward Weston's photograph, Tina closes her eyes for a fleeting moment as she recites poetry. And in Harry Callahan's, Eleanor surrenders to the water with eyes closed.

In her luminous phase, the She –Earth–, Gaia –Demeter– is fertile, docile and prodigious. But in her dark phase, she is associated with Dionysus or Zeus-Chthonius: the earth tremor.

Of what and of whom do these women dream? What tremor does their lapse in consciousness bring? What are they trying to say to us through the photographer's image?

•

This project reviews a series of nude, landscape and still-life photographs by Edward Weston (1886-1958) and Harry Callahan (1912-1999), two masters of modern American photography. My selection compares and contrasts iconic works by each man in order to identify common themes and strategies in their expressions of the erotic. Essentially, what I aim to prove is the existence of an erotic quality which, in becoming affective, transcends the presentation of the sexual motif, and which also extends to the depiction of natural objects or landscapes. More than a rhetoric of the sexual, these images seem to bring us face to face with an aesthetic of the erotic.

What defines this aesthetic? The first trait these images have in common is the fact that they depict people with whom the photographer had an affective bond –wives, lovers or children– and who work with him to produce the desired image. In addition to being "a nude of ...", the photographs are "a record of..." what, exactly? What do we, the spectators, see in the photographs of Weston and Callahan that inevitably causes us to interpret them as erotically charged?

Neither Weston nor Callahan spoke directly about the erotic component of their work. In both cases, they only admitted to having a formal, aesthetic intention. While Weston stated that he was "stimulated to work with the nude body, because of the infinite combinations of lines which are presented with every move"[1], Callahan held that "it's the subject matter that counts. I'm interested in revealing the subject in a new way to intensify it. A photo is able to capture a moment that people can't always see"[2]. With regard to the photographs of natural forms which viewers saw as sexually symbolic, Weston emphatically denied having any such intention:

> *Why were all these persons so profoundly affected on the physical side? For I can say with absolute honesty that not once while working with the shells did I have any physical reaction to them; nor did I try to record erotic symbolism. [...] I am not sick and I was never so free from sexual suppression. [...] I am not blind to the sensuous quality in shells, with which they combine the deepest spiritual significance: indeed it is this very combination of the physical and spiritual in a shell like the Chambered Nautilus, which makes it such an important abstract of life.*[3]

1   Edward Weston in Nancy Newhall (ed.), *The Daybooks of Edward Weston. II. California,* New York: Aperture, 1981, p. 12.

2   Harry Callahan, "Quotes by Harry Callahan", typescript, Tucson, Harry Callahan Archive, Center for Creative Photography (hereafter HC-CCP).

3   Weston in Newhall (ed.), op. cit., p. 32.

4   Nancy Newhall, "Edward Weston and the Nude", *Modern Photography* 16, no. 6, June 1952, pp. 38-43, 107-110.

5   *Studies of the Human Form by Two Masters: John Rawlings and Edward Weston*, New York: Maco, 1957.

6   Here the term "affective" is used in the sense of contemporary affect theory, as a liminal (*in-between-ness*), permeable condition that presupposes the capacity to act and be acted upon. Melissa Gregg and Gregory J. Seigworth (eds.), *The Affect Theory Reader*, Durham & London: Duke University Press, 2010, pp. 1-2.

1924 EDWARD WESTON

Weston's words are symptomatic of the problem we face when assessing the erotic component of his photographs: its consideration as both the effect and underlying cause of a physical condition means that it must be "suppressed" (repressed) even at the level of discourse. This is the reason why it is unavoidably associated with the spiritual: as in Romantic art, here we find a fusion of work, spirit and nature, which is also the basis for the mystified conception of the modern artist as a creative genius.

Weston's iconic photographs and, to a lesser extent, Callahan's as well, have generally been interpreted using these types of associations and assessments, which is why we must now re-examine them in a different light. In this case, my goal was to explore their images from the perspective of eroticism as a quality that blurs the distinctions between the traditional genres of the nude, the still life and the landscape. The idea is not new. Back in 1952, Nancy Newhall offered the first interpretation of Weston's nudes by associating them with his photographs of shells, peppers, seaweed and dunes. I say "first" because, prior to that year, only seven of the photographer's nudes had been published in monographs. Newhall attempted to remedy that situation by publishing an essay in *Modern Photography*[4], which was later followed by a longer book. While her essay on "Edward Weston and the Nude" was published in the magazine's June 1952 issue, the book never progressed beyond the mock-up stage, although an inexpensive, simplified version was eventually released together with John Rawlings' work a few months before Weston's death in January 1958.[5]

Ever since, the nudes of both Weston and Callahan are commonly presented alongside their photographs of natural forms. Although the justification for this association is the same given by Weston's first audiences –the *sensual-forms-as-erotic* argument– few have explored the function and meaning of this relationship. My selection attempts to go one step further, focusing on that obvious erotic component found in both photographers' work, but juxtaposing their images in an attempt to underscore something that is rarely discussed: the *affective* (binding, emotional, fluctuating and signifying) nature of the photographer-subject relationship as the basis of its erotic aesthetic.[6]

In order to understand this aesthetic, we must unravel the tangled knot of arguments normally used to explain these photos: those which, in order to suppress any mention of the erotic drive, explain the photographer's intention as a quest for form and composition, and those which sublimate the erotic drive by linking it to the intuitive and the spiritual. Both are repressive: the former obviates any discussion of sexual provocation as the photo's motivation and intention, while the latter denies the rationality of the photographer's compositional intent. As these arguments contradict and cancel each other out, the erotic quality becomes an aporia: composition is used as a pretext for denying the existence and expression of the sexual component, and the attempt to understand the sexual as spiritual

7   James Hillman, *The Myth of Analysis*, Evanston, IL: Northwestern University Press, 1972, p. 218.

8   Ibid., p. 219.

9   Gilles Mora, "Weston The Magnificent", *Edward Weston: Forms of Passion*, New York: Abrams, 1995, pp. 23-24.

is used as a pretext for concealing the active (conscious or unconscious) construction of that component.

What I want to show is that, beyond the photographers' receptiveness to the spirit of nature manifest in the woman, object or landscape before them, in both cases these elements evince a *malleability* which, in the case of the bodies, is revealed as an actively collaborative arrangement. If there is one thing that sets Weston and Callahan's nudes apart from other similar works, it is the *affective quality of their photographic language*: there is something in the images (the body, nature) that is permeable to us and renders us permeable in turn. Their aesthetic quality does not merely please us; it also changes us.

Although it would be absurd not to speak of the photographers, my intention here is to shift the focus from them to the images and, in particular, to their inter-subjective, performative language. Unlike images in which the photographer attempts to transform a subject into an erotic image (saying), in these photographs the subject seems to come forward to meet the photographer/spectator, forcing him to react. The image is the record of that encounter as an action (doing): a dialectical, collaborative game charged with erotic tension. This is the difference between a rhetoric and an aesthetic of the erotic: instead of describing the sexual subject, the images *sensibly* move us towards it.

The erotic quality derives from the performative use of photography: the image does not merely *speak* of the erotic, it constitutes an *erotic act*.

●

HE

First Adam, then Eve: in the narratives on which our gender values are based, She emerges from He. The biblical story is not all that different from the mythological account, which tells how Athena sprang from Zeus' head. Male primacy is established both genealogically and temporally: He is her material and formal cause, her precondition.[7]

The myth of the artist is not radically different from that of Adam: paradigmatically male, the artist is He who has the power to *create* by moulding inanimate material. In the traditional rendering, the *logos* (Apollo) acquires supremacy over the *physis* (Dionysus) which is associated with the female body: female, matter, evil, darkness and irrationality are understood as interchangeable concepts.[8] Although the formulation is Manichaean, the pertinent fact for our discussion is that the archetypal factor not only permeates the values of our male-female culture but also, and more specifically, the modern idea of the artist as creator traditionally used to explain Edward Weston and Harry Callahan.

I must point out that here I am speaking of the photographers themselves, not of their work. Like many other great photography masters, in the case of Weston and Callahan we observe a similar phenomenon: their work tends to be explained as a logical by-product of their personalities, rather than by attempting to analyse the sense and significance of their visual output.

Therein lies the true wellspring of Weston's organicism. Impelled by his deep-seated, visceral attraction to nature, organic forms proved an inexhaustible source of inspiration: not just vegetables, but the rocks, human beings and landscapes he considered organisms no less capable of participating in form's compelling revelation.[9]

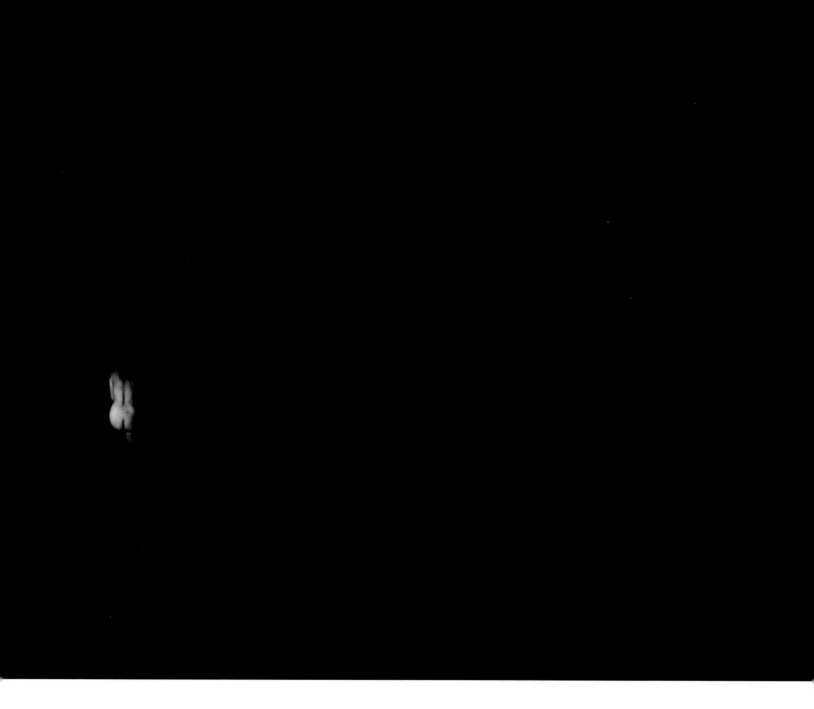

10 "Weston's pantheism mirrored the painter's metaphysical conception of the world and belief in Swedenborgian correspondences." Mora, ibid., p. 21.

11 Nancy Newhall (ed.), *The Daybooks of Edward Weston. I. Mexico II. California,* New York: Aperture, 1981, front endpaper.

12 Susan Sontag, *On Photography,* New York: Picador, 1977, p. 92.

13 Weston quoted in Newhall (ed.), *Daybooks,* p. XX.

14 Gilles Mora, "Weston in Mexico: A Testing Ground", *Edward Weston: Forms of Passion,* op. cit., p. 63.

Although this may be an insightful exegesis of Weston's photography, the similarity to that of Callahan makes us wonder if it has been formulated correctly or if it is tinged with a psychologism, romanticism or spiritualism similar to that found in the photographer's own writings, which betray the influence of Kandinsky's aesthetic *à la Swedenborg.*[10] Written intermittently between 1922 and 1944, Weston's *Daybooks* have been described as:

... an extraordinary document of the struggle of an artist to forge a style, to adjust himself to the world, to determine his position in society, and to appraise his contribution to it. [...] In many ways, the Daybooks *bring to mind Vincent van Gogh's letters to his brother Theo, which record the thoughts, feelings and inspirations of another great artist.*[11]

The text's intention is clear: to draw a parallel between Weston's and Van Gogh's diaries and so allow us to infer the artistic value of his photography. Like the previous quote, this excerpt also envelops Weston's work in a mystical aura: if it were merely a photographic record of reality –if a cabbage leaf is just a cabbage leaf and not a cloth, as described by Susan Sontag–[12] then it wouldn't be art. It is this register *according to XY* or *in the manner of XY* that marks the difference between an ordinary photograph and an art photograph. Here I feel I must underscore the maleness of artistic creation: as in the myths of Adam and Zeus, artistic creativity is yet another mystification of male action (*do we know of any female geniuses?*). In this case, the artistic value (the Artist as Creator) coincides with the condensed archetypal view of gender: even in the case of *women* artists like Modotti (note the necessary use of the epithet), their creativity is explained as having derived from–literally emerging *from the side of*–their male counterparts.

In this respect, it is interesting to note that both Weston and Callahan attempted to classify their work as art from the beginning of their careers. And over the years, they gradually shaped with their own personal definitions of photographic art. In the case of Weston, who had his first photo published in a magazine in 1903, at the tender age of 17, the process of defining a personal aesthetic entailed not only abandoning the pictorialist aesthetic of his first decade –even going so far as to burn his diaries and negatives– but also setting aside the sartorial trappings ("Windsor tie, green velvet jacket") he had once worn to proclaim his status as an artist. "One does not suddenly change", Weston believed. In his case, the catalyst of the shift towards a different notion of *artisticity* was his exposure to critical articles about Stieglitz's photographs published in the first decade of the 20th century:[13]

> *Increasingly, Weston was heeding the voice within. [...] He had broadened his cultural horizons by associating with artists from the West Coast and had come to the understanding that it was not enough to be a commercial craftsman, a mere professional photographer: he had to be an artist.*[14]

This conversion to art took place between 1923 and 1926 during his sojourn in Mexico. This also coincided with his relationship with Tina Modotti, whose husband, the painter Roubaix "Robo" de l'Abrie Richey, had organised an exhibition at the Academy of Fine Arts of Mexico in which Weston's work was featured. The favourable reviews–passed on by Tina–that Weston's art photography received and the possibility of being associated with the "Mexican Renaissance" movement were what led Weston to move to Mexico. There, thanks to his contact with artists such as Diego Rivera, Jean Charlot and David Alfaro Siqueiros, Weston received his first accolades and began forging his reputation a modern

15 Alfaro Siqueiros, "Una trascendental labor fotográfica. La exposición Weston-Modotti", *El Informador*, Guadalajara, 4 September 1925.

16 Jean Charlot, *Letter to Edward Weston*, 27 March 1925, Tucson, Edward Weston Archive, Center for Creative Photography (hereafter EW-CCP).

17 Edward Weston, *Daybooks*, Nancy Newhall (ed.), 1931, typescript, EW-CCP.

18 Nancy Newhall, "Edward Weston and the Nude", typescript, EW-CCP.

photographer. Siqueiros described the photography that Weston presented in Mexico in 1925 (alongside Modotti, by the way) in the following terms:

> *Weston and Modotti [...] make* TRUE PHOTOGRAPHIC BEAUTY. *The material qualities of the things and objects they portray could not be more* APT: *roughness is rough, smoothness is smooth, flesh is living, stone is hard. [...] In the sensation of reality imparted to spectators by the works of these two great masters, one must search for the* PLEASURE, *the* BEAUTY, THE PHOTOGRAPHIC AESTHETIC, *[...] a beauty that is absolutely modern.*[15]

With his use of capital letters, Siqueiros was emphasising what he believed constituted the modern photography aesthetic in Weston's work: the aesthetic value of realism and the artistic specificity of photography. In a letter written to Weston during his brief trip back to California in 1925, his friend Jean Charlot used the following arguments to convince him to hasten his return to Mexico:

> *Professionally, I think you can do better work here than in the States. Many tried to get by photograph the spirit of mechanic modern life, but you would be the first to try the spirit of simpleness and primitiveness by this medium. Your last things (birds, horse) were full of promise.*[16]

Charlot pointed out something that is rarely noted in connection with Weston's work: the fact that it was during his Mexican sojourn, and in the course of the assignment he received from Anita Brenner to photograph traditional Mexican handicrafts for *Mexican Folkways*, when the association between simple object and "pure" form first appeared in his work. This is evident in photographs like *Two Birds - Gourds* (1925), whose abstract purism predated that of his photos of vegetables, shells and natural forms. On this topic, I would like to highlight the contradiction between the rhetoric used in formal-artistic assessments of Weston's work (photography = modernity, simplicity) and the vibrant terms in which the photographer explained his own output:

> *What is the difference between the "presentation" I would make of a cabbage and that made by the commercial man? The latter with matter-of-fact approach sees a cabbage as an unrelated fact, devoid of interest except as a means to* sauerkraut. *I feel in the same cabbage, all the mystery of life force. I am amazed, emotionally stirred, and by my way of presentation, my recognition of the reasons for the cabbage form, its significance in relation to all forms, I am able to communicate my experience to others.*[17]

In his statement of intent, the photographer speaks of his work as an epiphany (a "vision"), not as the result of a rational and deliberate exercise in formal, abstract composition. Thus, in his writings Weston defines his work as a "presentation" (his realist and synthetic compositions) rather than an "interpretation" (his pictorialist images with their metaphorical aura). Newhall described this change as "a passage through the blind alley of the Abstract into the Real".[18]

In Harry Callahan's case, it was Ansel Adams who inspired his idea of photography as art. Listening to a series of talks that Adams gave at the Detroit Camera Club in 1941 encouraged him to do something similar to what Weston had done: abandon the early pictorialist style he had embraced as a member of the Camera Club:

> *Later on, after I'd seen what other people did in the camera club, I got these things that looked kind of good to me. But I felt kind of frustrated, things seemed all wrong.*

19 Robert Brown, "Harry M. Callahan Interview", *Archives of American Art*, 13 February 1975, [http://www.americansuburbx.com/2012/12/theory-harry-m-callahan-interview-feb.html] 2/02/2013.

20 Harry Callahan, "Landscape Book 3-23-80", typescript, Harry Callahan Archive, Center for Creative Photography (HC-CCP).

21 Brown, ibid.

22 Harry Callahan, ibid.

23 Harry Callahan cited by Britt Salvesen, *Harry Callahan: The Photographer at Work*, Tucson, The Center for Creative Photography / Yale University Press, 2006, p. 25 (original citation in Ann Parson, "Harry Callahan," Boston Phoenix Magazine, October 19, 1976, p. 6.

24 Brown, ibid.

[...] Then Ansel Adams came. He showed his work and it was all straight photography–sharp and beautiful prints and everything else, and that just completely set me free.[19]

However, Adams and Callahan were interested in very different subject matters: while Adams sought spectacular landscapes, Callahan felt that he could photograph "walls or whatever was available in the midwest. [...] Ansel freed me to photograph the non-spectacular. I thought I could make a footprint in the sand that would stand as an abstraction of a sand dune in the west"[20]. Like Weston, Callahan started out working with large-format cameras (a 4x5 Linhof Technika and an 8x10 Deardorff for which he traded his enlarger), which he used to obtain contact copies of incredible detail and "photographic beauty", like Adams' and Weston's:

The camera was a machine and it could make machine-like pictures which were very beautiful. [...] It could get such texture–you know, that was just magnificent to me, and I immediately got a bigger camera. I got an eight-by-ten camera, and just contact-printed my pictures because that was the sharpest you could get. [...] That's a real weird thing. [...] I just look at something and first I think I see how sharp it is. It's something to do with the lens. [...] We got interested in Weston then, and so we sort of did West Coast pictures. In Detroit, right...[21]

Callahan's use of the first-person plural is a reference to his friend and fellow photographer Todd Webb, his travelling companion in those years (just as Weston had been Adams'). And, like Weston, Callahan was heavily influenced by Stieglitz's photographs: "Besides Ansel Adams, the photographer who had an enormous influence on me was Stieglitz. He was always up there in the clouds, but he was talking about life, and searching for the truth"[22]. Stieglitz's *Equivalents* (*Music, A Sequence of Ten Cloud Photographs*, 1922) and Adams' series of waves (*Surf Sequence*, 1941) both inspired his series of water photos. In this project, and despite the admiration he felt for Adams, he began to break the rules that Ansel had established. Instead of carefully retaining the texture in light and shadow, Callahan "burned" his negatives by overexposing and over-developing them. And so he developed his trademark style:

One of the big steps in my photography was when I photographed weeds in the snow. I´d heard all Ansel´s talk about texture, tone, and how an orange filter improves snow´s texture, but all of a sudden a picture I had taken looked wonderful with no texture at all. I wasn't conscious of anything while I was photographing, but when I got home I found that by printing it with a great deal of contrast, I had discovered something.[23]

Callahan describes his process in technical terms but, like Weston, he does not mention any deliberate order or composition. The image seems to be a product of the photographer's ability to vitally connect with his subject: like Weston, Callahan describes himself as a kind of thaumaturge. It is rather paradoxical that Callahan distinguished himself as a teacher for years, and yet in his discourse the rational, intentional effort of composition is ultimately subsumed under the epiphanic vision of the Romantic artist: a combination of technical struggle and vision, the image seems to be resolved by some inexpressible means, by a flash of intuition:[24]

Sometimes I would tell the graduate students that I felt that they were giving themselves a grant. That´s why I said that they had two years to do the things they wanted to do. So the people who really liked to photograph did it. I can´t figure out why my

25 Harry Callahan, "Statement", typescript, HC-CCP.

26 "Chronology by Dolores A. Knapp",
typescript, HC-CCP.

27 Britt Salvesen, *op. cit.*, p. 38.

28 Sontag, *op. cit.*, p. 100.

teaching worked. I really can´t. I mean I can´t say what makes a picture, so how can I say I can communicate with somebody.[25]

At the age of 33, in 1945, Callahan had such confidence in his artistic abilities that he left his job as a lab technician in Detroit and awarded himself a "personal fellowship" to go and live in New York. There he met Berenice Abbott, Paul Strand, Lisette Model and the Newhalls. And three years later (at 36, the same age Weston was when he travelled to Mexico) he met Edward Steichen, with whom he would establish "one of the most meaningful relationships of his life"[26]. Steichen was destined to be instrumental in Callahan's career; the very year they met, he included the photographer in two shows at the MoMA, and he later featured his work in such influential exhibitions as *Diogenes with a Camera I* (1952) and *The Family of Man* (1955).

By that time Callahan had moved back to the Midwest, to Chicago, where he embarked on a lengthy teaching career at the Institute of Design, the "New Bauhaus" founded by Moholy-Nagy in 1937. In the 1950s Callahan and Aaron Siskind taught side-by-side at the Institute of Design, developing a critical camaraderie that supported and nourished the best years of his creative output.

Although Britt Salvesen sustains that the two men adopted opposing strategies –Callahan attempted to arrive at the idea via his reaction to the world, while Siskind subordinated his reaction to the concept–[27] this opposition is only superficial. On commenting that "when I make a photograph, I want it to be an altogether new object, complete and self-contained, whose basic condition is order"[28], Siskind seems to be referring not only to his photographs but also to those of Callahan and Weston.

Despite certain parallels between their lives as artists (travel and encounters with other artists as turning points in their work) and the similarity of their discourses (the shared rhetoric of the photographic "vision" as a freeze-frame of the subject's *essence*), the overlap between Weston and Callahan's oeuvres is most obvious in their shared intention of formal order. By speaking of an epiphany-like *presentation* rather than of *representation*, both refuse to consider photographic composition as a rational and necessary factor for the construction of the image: if there is an erotic aesthetic in the image, it is merely a by-product of the object's own qualities, not of any conscious intention or expression achieved through his work of composition.

In the creation of He –the epiphanic image of order and control– the erotic quality is incidental. The tremor, the erotic drive, is foisted off on the subject: on the earth, nature, woman.

•

SHE

Diana, goddess and huntress, undresses to bathe.

Emerging from a woodland grove, Actaeon, man and hunter, stumbles upon her: he is captivated by her beauty.

Feeling that her divine body has been profaned, she punishes him by turning him into a stag: "Now you may tell, if you can tell, that is, of having seen me naked!"

Actaeon flees, but he is pursued and torn to pieces by his own hounds–fifty of them, according to Ovid's tale.

Chiron hears the baleful lament of Actaeon's hounds and creates a statue of their master to calm and console them. Image as exorcism.

•

1935 EDWARD WESTON

29   Weston quoted in Newhall (ed.), *Daybooks II*, p. 45.

30   John Paul Caponigro interviews Harry Callahan, quoted in David Travis, "There Are Two Sides to Every Picture", in *The Archive 35. Harry Callahan: Variations on a Theme*, Tucson, Center for Creative Photography, October 2007, p. 36.

31   Sontag, ibid., pp. 14-15.

32   It was not until the 17th century that the female body began to be considered more attractive than the male body. Kenneth Clark, *El desnudo*, Madrid, Alianza Forma, 1984, p. 78 [Original title: *The Nude*].

33   Nancy Newhall, "Edward Weston and the Nude", typescript, 1952, EW-CCP.

The myth of Actaeon allows us to examine what occurs in the photos of Weston and Callahan in a different light. Both are almost obsessively concerned with the form and texture of their subjects, but they avoid mentioning the pleasure of the gaze, something that is obviously experienced when contemplating a naked body, especially that of a female beloved. In Weston we perceive his need to conceal his lovers' identities (or to downplay his fame as a Don Juan, mentioned by several of his friends),[29] whereas in Callahan, his primary concern seems to be his wife's public image and reputation.:

> *She was innocent and I was innocent. I just try to photograph what I like. I thought she was beautiful. I intuitively photographed her. All my photography is innocent.*[30]

The nude is just another genre, and the body is merely a subject. And yet –as Susan Sontag so eloquently explained when discussing the predatory nature of the photographic act– [31] it has all the air of a hunt: He, the photographer/hunter, devises tactics in order to trap the image of Her, the naked prey, in the snare of his camera.

Weston and Callahan defend their nude photography with the same argument used throughout art history: we are not seeing a naked body but a canonical form that was defined in the 5th century BC: the Nude. The ideal dimensions of this form are fundamental: equated with reason or proportion in Greek art, the perfection of the body implies mediation between the human and the divine. Men admire the nude bodies of the perfect gods because they do not decay over time like their own (here it is important to remember that the Greeks actually preferred the male body to the female form).[32] The divine form exorcises any embarrassment or shame one might feel when gazing upon it. We have traditionally required veils of innocence in order to contemplate the nude: stories from the Bible or classical mythology have served as the pretext for allowing Western spectators to freely contemplate the naked bodies of goddesses, saints or nymphs. Protected by the form, the spectator recognises the characters: this is Eve, that is Venus, over there is Susannah, that one is Salome. But what he sees is the body.

Thus, it is no coincidence that Weston and Callahan's early nudes resemble the ideal forms of the Nude: in Weston's first nude portrait of his wife, taken in 1909, she is cast in the role of Eve. Flora, just a few months into her first pregnancy, poses naked in a bucolic setting, lifting her arm as if to pluck a piece of fruit from a tree. The resulting image is exquisite, elegant, pictorialist: an ideal female form encoded in a biblical representation.

In the early nudes of both photographers, we see the woman's entire body portrayed against the space. The idea is that of a theatre: a figure against a stage. And –most importantly– a part to be played: the naked bodies serve an allegorical function of *this as that*. Flora *as* Eve, Eleanor *as* the artist's model. In both cases, the nude body operates as a metaphor associated with myths: with a biblical story that has defined our current gender values, in Weston's case, and with the 19th-century artistic trope of the model in the artist's studio, in Callahan's.

In the first attempt to formulate an exegesis of Weston's nudes –the aforementioned 1952 text by Nancy Newhall– these myths were, as convention dictated, associated with the Western allegorical tradition:

> *[But for equal] thousands of years, artists have kept returning to the Nude because it is fundamental and vital. [...] They have covered walls with Hercules and ceilings with Venus, and churches with everything from Adam and Eve to Susannah and the Elders. They have used the Nude as a symbol juxtaposed with other symbols; they have mined in the subterranean vistas of Freud.*[33]

34 Edward Weston in Newhall (ed.), *Day-books*, pp. 26-27.

35 Nancy Newhall, "Edward Weston and the Nude", pp. 1-2.

Why does Newhall feel the need to justify Weston's nudes in this way? Why does she only obliquely refer to the unconscious erotic potential of nude images (although later in the text she denies that this applies to Weston's photos)? This text was written in 1952 to accompany the publication of his nudes in *Modern Photography*, a widely read magazine. It is common knowledge that mainstream society in 1950's America was anything but morally permissive, and Newhall feared attracting criticism and disapproval. Only in Mexico had Weston felt confident enough to show his most realistic, explicit nudes, such as those taken in California before his 1923 trip. These photos had been enthusiastically received, earning Weston the respect and admiration of the Mexican art community.

> *Nothing has pleased me more than Rivera's enthusiasm. [...] Looking at the sand in one of my beach nudes, a torso of Margrethe, he said, "This is what some of us 'moderns' were trying to do when we sprinkled real sand on our paintings or stuck on pieces of lace or paper or other bits of realism." [...] Of the eight prints sold, six were nudes of Margrethe made that last terrific week with her, before leaving for Mexico. Rivera liked one of the beach fragments of her the best of anything in my collection.*[34]

Although, by the time he met Weston, Diego Rivera was one of the leading exponents of post-revolutionary Mexican muralism, in his European phase the painter had flirted with abstraction and Cubism, which explains why he preferred those formalist, abstract nudes of Margrethe. In these pictures the ideal of the nude as theatre was shattered and replaced by the image of a real body, generally fragmented: the torso as a graphic form against the background. Adopted by Callahan himself, too, this strategy would ultimately become one of his style´s trademarks.

If, in attempting to understand the images' evolution towards an erotic aesthetic, we only heed the *logical* explanation of the photographers (or of art history), we could simply explain it as a shift in plastic strategies: on the formal level, Weston and Callahan drew closer to the body to render it more abstract; and on the thematic level, they moved away from the allegorical or iconographic tropes of their early images. However, if we apply the knowledge of our perceptive instincts, we will inevitably sense the appearance of an erotic, aesthetic *something more*: a factor that is suppressed in the photographers' rhetoric and is associated with the lusty sensuality of the form. Our *psychological* comprehension confirms the existence of an erotic drive in the perfect nudes of Weston and Callahan, an impression that becomes increasingly stronger as the photographer reduces the physical distance between him and his model. Thus, the nudes with fragmented bodies invoke an undeniable proximity to the body of the other, the same closeness we interpret as an acutely intimate situation.

Can a photographer not have an emotional response to a live nude body? And is it possible for the spectator not to have an analogous reaction? Although Nancy Newhall does not mention the unmistakable eroticisation of the photographer's gaze in her text, she does hint at this possibility:

> *The artist confronted by the Nude is as naked psychologically as his model in actuality. The painter's sleight-of-hand can no more conceal behind a convenient flutter of drapery who he is, at what stage of growth, and where his imagination halts, than the photographer can hide behind his camera, which has always revealed who is behind it more mercilessly than who is in front.*[35]

Faced with the nakedness of the woman posing for him, Weston reacts with an aesthetic affection that might also be emotional, for he was intimately involved with practically all

36 Edward Weston quoted in Jessica Todd Smith, "Time of Exposure: Nancy Newhall's Unpublished Book of Edward Weston's Nudes", in VV.AA., *Edward Weston: A Legacy*, London: Merrell, 2003, p. 83.

37 Weston in Newhall (ed.), *Daybooks II*, p. 17.

38 Ibid., p. 210.

39 Harry Callahan, "Slide presentation. Shepherd College. April 8, 1981", typescript, HC-CCP.

40 Although he started out with an 8x10" camera, Weston ended up switching to a 4x5 (9x12 cm) Graflex. In the early days, Callahan used an 8x10 (20x25 cm) Deardorff, but he later used 6x6 cm negatives.

41 Harry Callahan, "Slide presentation", ibid.

42 Todd, op. cit., p. 96.

of the women he portrayed. Although only two of them were official wives (Flora Chandler and Charis Wilson), Weston made no secret about living with Tina Modotti and Sonya Noskowiak, and he was also romantically involved with Anita Brenner, Miriam Lerner, Cristel Gang, Bertha Wardell and Sybil Anakeef, among others.[36] Consequently, although he liked to think of his own photography in purely formal terms ("a direct response to form", as he once confessed to Henrietta Shore),[37] at some point he had to admit that these women were an important source of inspiration for him:

> To really blossom, one must feel wanted, loved: must feel a place is open for one's especial capacity–not just any job. [...] There must be balance –giving and receiving– of equal import whether in sex or art.[38]

Callahan's nudes feature only one woman, his wife, Eleanor, and later–but only as a young girl–his daughter Barbara. Although they seem to be lost in thought in the images, it is obvious that they are collaborating with their husband/father: only that trusting, loving surrender could have produced these seemingly fluid photographs which nevertheless boast the extraordinary precision and sharpness of the large-format image:

> This is about as arty of a snapshot as you can get. I really don't remember of any motivation here other than I really wanted to photograph Eleanor in a lot of different backgrounds and techniques. I had to keep working at whatever one it was until something worked. I keep saying "work", but it´s not work to me, because it´s something I really wanted to do..[39]

Callahan refers to a large-format photograph as a "snapshot"; like Weston, he sought to convey the sensation of the flowing nature of life, but with *precision*. They both faced the same problem when working with models: the difficulty of freezing a movement with large, heavy cameras that required long exposure times.[40] When Weston described his work with the dancer Bertha Wardell, he mentioned exposure times of one-fifth of a second, whereas Eleanor's poses for Callahan's photos had to be held for as long as 20 seconds:

> I really got a bing bang out of photographing Eleonor and Barbara in this kind of light of our living room. I was photographing Eleanor and I thought, well, I would like to photograph towards the light with the 8x10 camera, and it was a twenty second exposure, and while I liked the picture that twenty second exposure really fot me. She sat through the whole thing.[41]

Posing always entails certain difficulties, but sitting for Weston and Callahan was a highly complicated undertaking. Without the speed of the instant camera, the photographer and his model had to find a synergistic choreography that would allow both freedom and freezing of movement. Weston explained his strategy in the following way:

> This series of 4x5 nudes was made without any instructions to the models (I never use professionals, just my friends) as to what they should do. I would say, "Move around all you wish to, the more the better." Then when something happened, I would say, "Hold it." And things did happen all the time.[42]

According to Charis Wilson, his second wife and model, Weston's idea of "moving around freely" was more like something "you might do if you were trying to slip out of your bed

43 Charis Wilson and Wendy Madar, *Through Another Lens: My Years with Edward Weston*, New York: Farrar, Straus & Giroux, 1998, p. 10.

44 Ibid., p. 11.

45 Letter from Bertha Wardell dated 25 March 1927, quoted by Weston in Newhall (ed.), *Daybooks II*, p. 11.

46 Edward Weston, *Daybooks*, manuscript, p. 36, EW-CCP.

without disturbing a sleeping rattlesnake". Posing was not a relaxed procedure, as for her part she tried to "visualise and enhance the image I was transmitting". [43] Charis described Weston's movements from her perspective as a model:

> He could adjust the focus by reaching around to the front of the camera while looking into the hood. Sometimes he moved the tripod slightly without lifting his head, and I imagined he was a five-legged creature from another world whose giant eye was insatiably curious about this one. But I decided at once that the metaphor was false; creatures from other worlds were clumsy in my imagining, and Edward's dance with his camera was remarkably graceful. [44]

Very few of the artists' models have left written testimonies of their experience, making Charis' lengthy memoirs particularly valuable. Written in her old age, many years after her divorce from Weston, once he had already made his reputation as a master of modern photography, her book *Through Another Lens: My Life with Edward Weston* is a candid, first-hand source of information about the photographer's private life. But it is also a symptomatic example of the female condition experienced *through* a man, which feminist critics would consider a social pathology. And perhaps it is to a degree, if we consider that Bertha Wardell described her experience with Weston in similar terms:

> You seemed possessed for an instant not only of a physical but of a psychical fatigue. [...] What you do awakes in me so strong a response that I must in all joy tell you. Your photographs are as definite an experience to the spirit as a whip lash to the body. It is as if they said, "Look –here is something you have been waiting for– something you have not found in painting nor even in sculpture, something which has been before only in the thought of dancing". [45]

This letter, Weston noted, indicates why he would work more with her. And his collaboration with Wardell led not only to an intensely passionate romance but to many of Weston's iconic nudes. In these images, Wardell's body folds itself docilely, sensibly and sensually, but it is always fragmented and headless:

> B. sat to me again: six negatives exposed, all of some value, three outstanding, but two of the latter slightly moved. However, the one technically good is the one best seen. As she sat with legs bent under, I saw the repeated curve of thigh and calf –the shin bone, knee and thigh lines forming shapes not unlike great sea shells– the calf curved across the upper leg, the shell's opening. [46]

More than a detailed representation of the body itself, the result of which might be an aseptic formalism –or outright pornography– what we perceive as erotic is the surgical discovery of the body through visual examination. This sensual or sexual quality does not stem from its formal, abstract, fragmentary nature but from the photographic act, which emulates the physical searching of the body conducted by the photographer/spectator. Though in Weston's case the fragmentation has more to do with the need to protect his models' identity than with formal aims, its effect is always the same: that of a gaze constructed through the act of searching.

> To scrutinise *means* to search: *I am searching the other's body, as if I wanted to see what was inside it, as if the mechanical cause of my desire were in the adverse body (I am like those children who take a clock apart in order to find out what time is).*

47 Roland Barthes, *A Lover's Discourse*, New York: Hill and Wang, 2001, p. 71.

48 Roland Barthes, *Sade, Fourier, Loyola*, New York: Hill and Wang, 1976, pp. 26-27.

49 The theory of the gaze as a power relationship between a male observer and a female object posited by John Berger in 1972 and, more specifically, by Laura Mulvey in 1975, has since been refuted by Norman Bryson (gaze as control) and Steve Neale (objectivisation of the male body), among others. John Berger, *Ways of Seeing*, Hammonsworth: Penguin, 1972; Laura Mulvey, "Visual Pleasure and Narrative Cinema", *Screen*, vol. 15, no. 3, 1975, pp. 6-18; Norman Bryson, *Vision and Painting: The Logic of the Gaze*, Princeton: Yale University Press, 1983, p. 94; Steve Neale, "Masculinity as Spectacle: Reflections on Men and Mainstream Cinema", *Screen*, vol. 24, no. 6, 1983; pp. 2-16;

This operation is conducted in a cold and astonished fashion; I am calm, attentive, as if I were confronted by a strange insect of which I am suddenly no longer afraid.[47]

This description of the gaze given by Roland Barthes in "The Other's Body" is pertinent because it sheds light on the motivation behind the cold and astonished scrutiny of the other's body: to identify the observer's desire by searching the body of the other. The erotic potential of Weston and Callahan's apparently cold, objective nudes does not lie in the representation of a theme –a torso, breast, pubis or sex– but in the *quality of the photographic action* which creates that representation. Putting it more clearly: what excites us about these images is not their extreme realism (pornography is explicit and not necessarily erotic) but the *control over the body* manifested in its subjection to scrutiny. As Barthes himself explains in connection with Sade, there can be no eroticism without reason or measure: in other words, without philosophising, dissertation, harangue or *logos*. Sadian passion is a system of articulated language with precise rules governing each action. From the combination of those actions emerges a new language, a "code" of love, as elaborate as that of courtly love.[48] As we deduce from the photographers' writings, there is something cold and mechanical about how they handle their subject, the body. Yet, as Barthes explains, that very act of exercising reason and control over the body is the source of its eroticism.

This perspective is interesting because it allows us to understand the contradictory nature of Weston and Callahan's nudes: the coexistence within them of diametrically opposed qualities such as formal coldness and erotic sensuality. Barthes' text also suggests the possibility that the direction of the gaze might be reversed. Beneath the voyeur's pleasure (Freudian *scopophilia*) and its implicit objectivisation of the scrutinised person (Sadian passion or Mulvey's "gaze")[49] lies something that subverts the power relationship: the fear that is born of desire itself and traps the gazer in its clutches.

Poetic and subjective, Barthes' text allows us to look beyond the conventional interpretation of the gaze. There is undoubtedly a scrutinising gaze that "objectifies" the woman portrayed (especially when her image is fragmented), and among women there is also a form of self-imposed objectivisation. Charis, Bertha and Tina see themselves how Weston sees them: as beautiful, sensual, sexual objects, as *objets d'art*. Eleanor also –we assume– approved of the images taken by her husband, as they were widely and publicly exhibited.

But in addition to sharing a perspective that explains the gaze as masculine and objectivising (Laura Mulvey), Barthes' text adds another interesting twist to the issue: as a response to his scrutiny, the photographer/spectator must face his own desire. That which was gazed upon (the other's body) returns *the gaze* as a force that inverts the power relationship: Is it truly He who has the power, controlling/representing with the gaze? Or is it She, the apparently passive one, who by the quality of her presence determines what can or cannot be done with her body?

The gaze goes from being an action with sadistic connotations –Sontag's hunter– to another narcissistic or masochistic projection –Barthes' gaze–. The direction of the gaze alternates between the two poles, blurring the distinction between roles: the subject becomes object, and the active-male becomes passive-female. The observer uses the other's body to find his own desire, and the observed uses the observer in order to see his own sex (narcissism). Beyond desire, in the gaze there is a fascination with the abyss of sex (masochism) or a horror or sense of guilt over deficiency, smallness or insignificance (obsession with castration or mutilation).

The erotic image is a battlefield: a *mise-en-scène* of the inter-subjective, reciprocal, binding game of the gaze. An eye that affects and allows itself to be affected by what is seen.

50 This oscillation between rhetoric and erotics was inspired by Susan Sontag's final demand in *Against Interpretation*, where she stated that in place of a hermeneutics of art (interpretation) we need an erotics of art. This is, in my opinion, precisely what Roland Barthes does in *A Lover's Discourse*. Susan Sontag, *Against Interpretation*, New York,: Dell Publishing, 1966; Roland Barthes, ibid.

51 It was after seeing Henrietta Shore's paintings of sea shells that Weston began to photograph them in his studio. Weston in Newhall (ed.), *Daybooks II*, op. cit., p. 17. See also Roger Aikin, "Henrietta Shore and Edward Weston", *American Art*, vol. 6, no. 1, Winter 1992; pp. 41-61.

52 Tina Modotti quoted by Weston in Newhall (ed.), ibid., p.

It takes two to construct desire through vision.
Actaeon, the hunter, is hunted down.

●

IT

Imagining him to be a monster, Psyche breaks the promise she made to her unknown husband, who pays her amorous visits each night under cloak of darkness. On lighting a lamp to see him, she loses him: he was the lovely Eros, one of whose arrows wounds her.

In order to recover Eros, Aphrodite orders Psyche to complete a series of tasks. Her final task is to descend into Hades, the underworld: she must obtain the secret beauty ointment of Persephone, queen of the underworld and daughter of Demeter, the Earth.

Psyche manages to get around Cerberus, Persephone's fierce guard dog, but she fails upon opening the box of ointment and pouring the contents over herself: it is none other than the deep slumber of Hades from which Eros, in turn, must now rescue her.

●

Seeing-as-pleasure

One thing is clear in the nudes and photographs of natural objects of Weston and Callahan, and that is that they function as stimulants of visual pleasure. Hence their erotic dimension, which has more to do with the myriad imaginative processes that the images trigger than with the representation of themes which are sexually explicit in and of themselves. More than a rhetoric, we find ourselves facing an erotics of the image.

The distinction between the two is important: while rhetoric focuses on the choice of subjects and their explicit description, erotics emanates from the imaginary qualities of the image, as Barthes suggested. It is a language constructed *out of* and *around* sex as a function, not as a subject.[50]

What I would like to prove here is that, although Weston and Callahan's photography has been evaluated as the product of a logical psyche, it can also been seen in the light of an erotic psyche. In this respect, it is not surprising that the first observers to notice the erotic dimension of Weston's photos were women: Henrietta Shore, Tina Modotti and Nancy Newhall. For while Weston, by 1927, had already produced industrial and craft-related forms in Mexico with symbolic connotations (his *Excusado* or *Toilet*, for example), it was Shore, back in California, who opened his eyes to the suggestive power of natural forms. The similarity between Shore's shell paintings and Weston's photographs is striking. Shore was also the first to harshly criticise Weston's fragmented nudes; in her view, by repeating the motif he was becoming too used to it and losing his sense of amazement.[51] Tina, for her part, could not suppress her physical reaction to Weston's shell photos in Mexico when she received them:

> When I opened the package I couldn't look at them very long, they stirred up all my innermost feelings so that I felt a physical pain. [...] I cannot look at them too long without feeling exceedingly perturbed, they disturbed me not only mentally but physically. There is something so pure and at the same time so perverse about them. They contain both the innocence of natural things and the morbidity of a sophisticated, distorted mind. They make me think of lilies and of embryos. They are mystical and erotic.[52]

We would be hard pressed to find a better description of *affect* than this. Tina provides a valuable clue to understanding the eroticism of Weston's photographs of natural forms, which can also be applied to Callahan's work: the association of these forms with the irrational, visceral and uncontrollable force of nature, which is also the creative force.

The images address the psyche in its mother tongue: the language of emotion, drama, sensuality, fantasy. The truth of the image does not exist, because on the imaginary plane we do not perceive objects, only meanings. The image is also the gateway to It, to Hades, the Unconscious: whither Psyche must venture to recover Eros.

Darkness and unconsciousness: Hades –the It, the dark– is also Physis, nature. Physis and Psyche represent antithetical and complementary forces: by plunging like Psyche into the irrational, uncontrollable force of nature, we become part of a whole. There is no longer any I, nor you: all is sensation. Plunging into the It opens the door to a new kind of power, of knowledge; we define our experiences in fields where words are inadequate (sight comes before speech). In the world of images there are no dreams, no morals, emotions or sense of time. It is in that world of *affect* –of allowing ourselves to be transformed by the other or the Other It– where we feel the multiplicity and complexity of our psychic experience: the desire –and the vertigo– of becoming subjects by way of another.

The true object of these images taken by Edward Weston and Harry Callahan is not the body but desire. Their work is photography as an affective and reflective act: perhaps more sexual in Weston, perhaps more loving in Callahan. But in the end, both bodies of work pass the erotic drive over to the It, the Whole: the irrational force and all-encompassing whole of a nature that is born, reproduces and dies, and that lives within and outside us. And it also has the power to be reborn, both materially and psychically: through the symbol, erotic energy is transmuted into images.

Seen in this light, the photography of Weston and Callahan is an invitation into the abyss: that abyss which is nothing but the vertigo of the sublime.

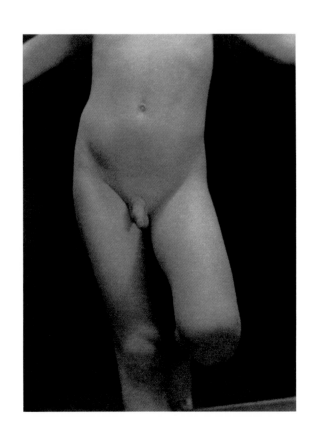

1923 EDWARD WESTON

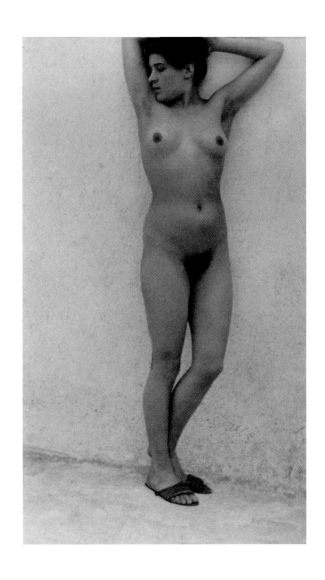

1950 HARRY CALLAHAN

1978 HARRY CALLAHAN

1948 HARRY CALLAHAN

1954 HARRY CALLAHAN

1954 HARRY CALLAHAN

HARRY CALLAHAN

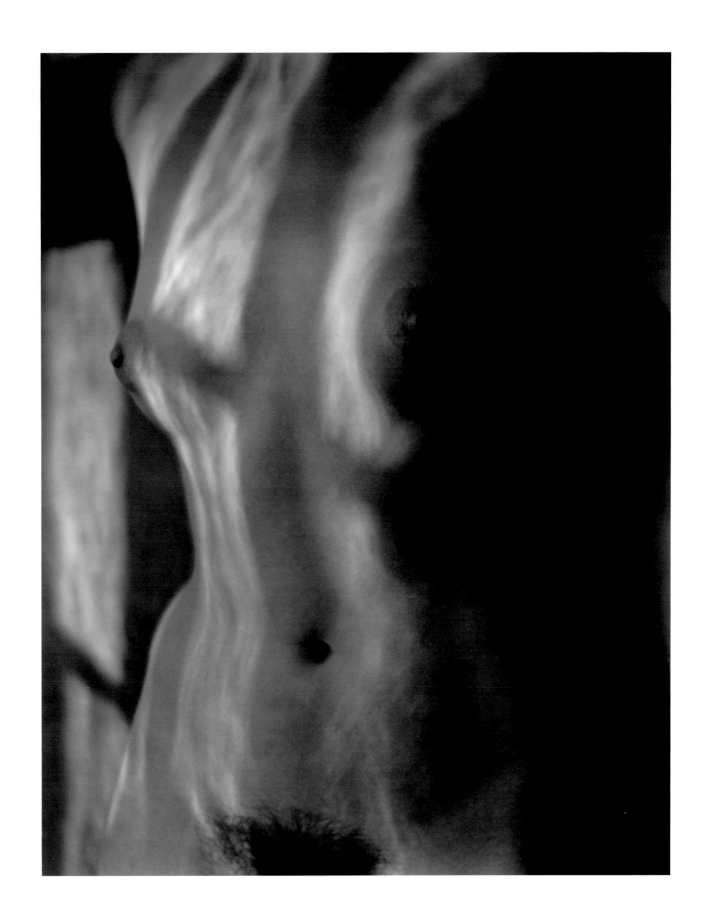

ca.1954 Harry Callahan

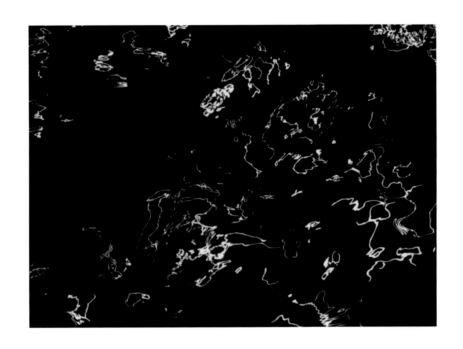

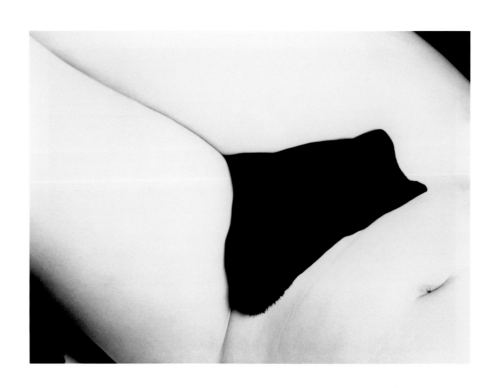

1947 HARRY CALLAHAN

1935 EDWARD WESTON

59

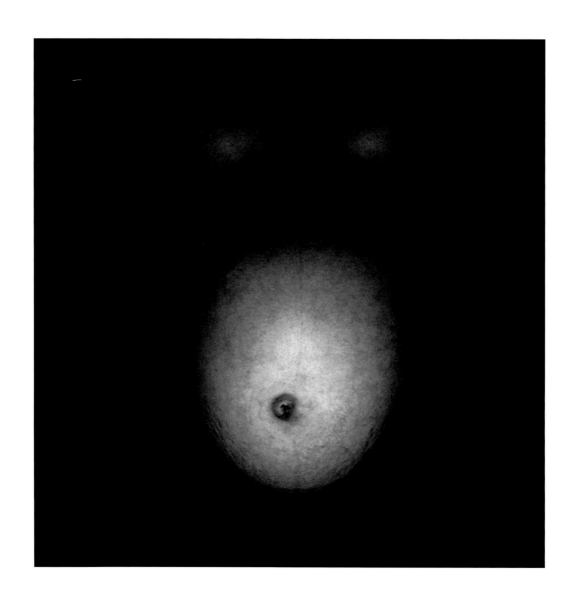

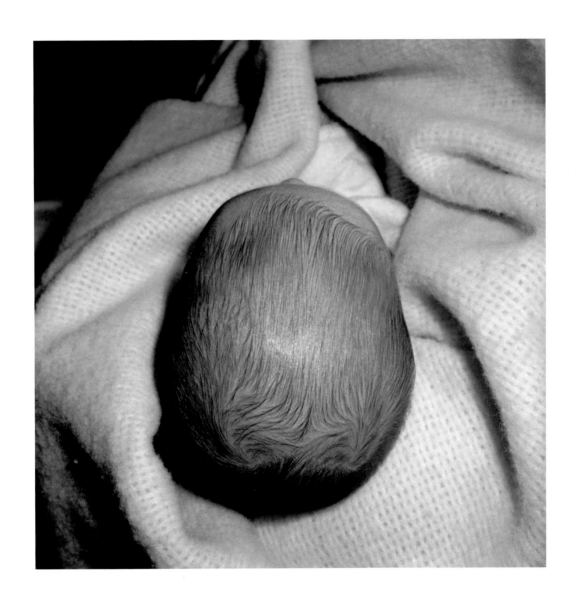

1948 Harry Callahan

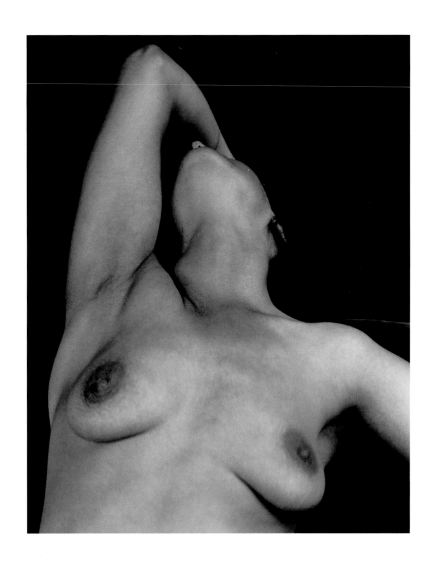

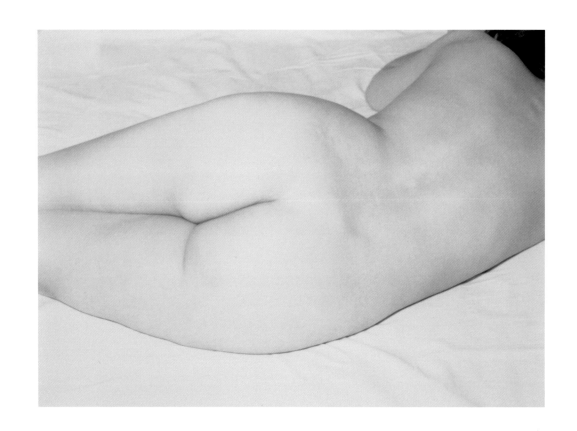

ca.1949 HARRY CALLAHAN

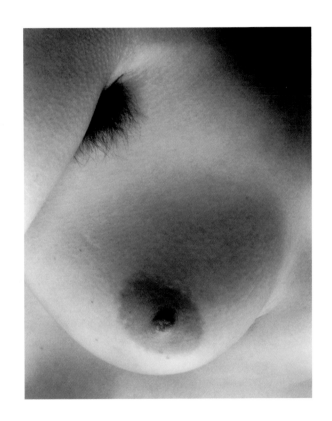

1936Edward Weston

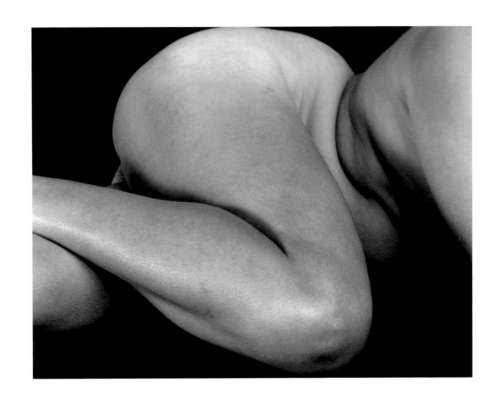

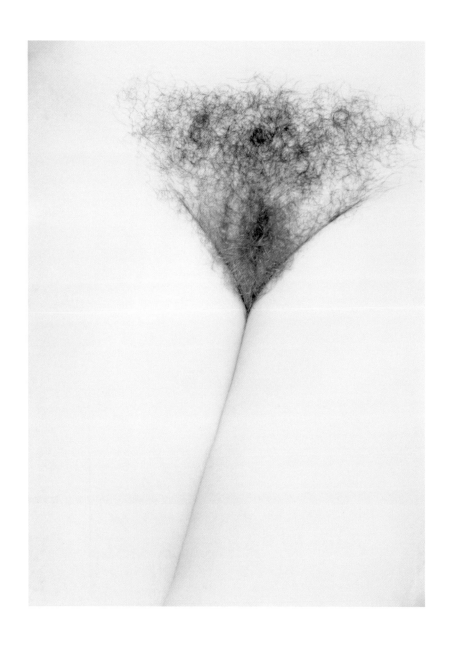

ca.1948 HARRY CALLAHAN

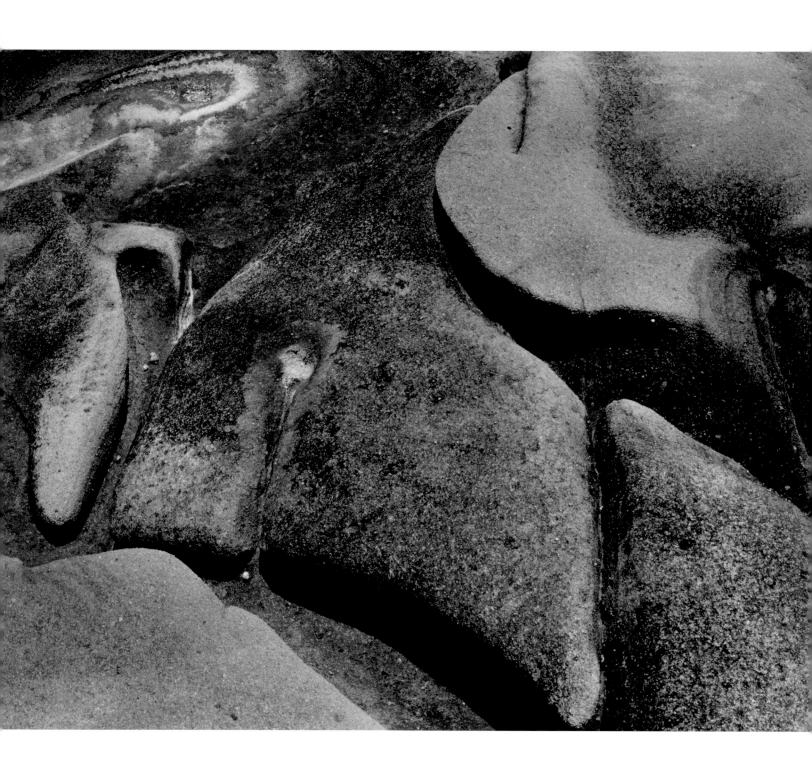

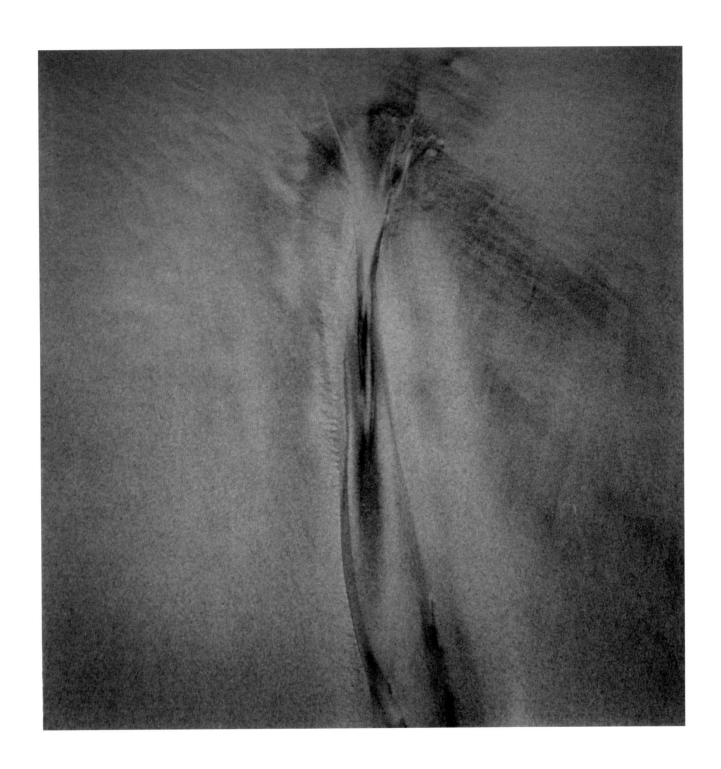

1948 HARRY CALLAHAN

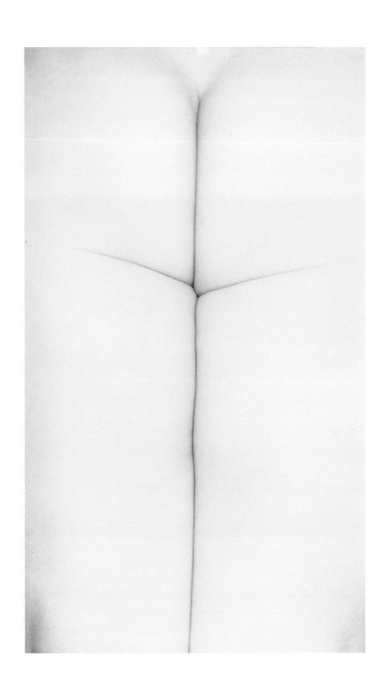

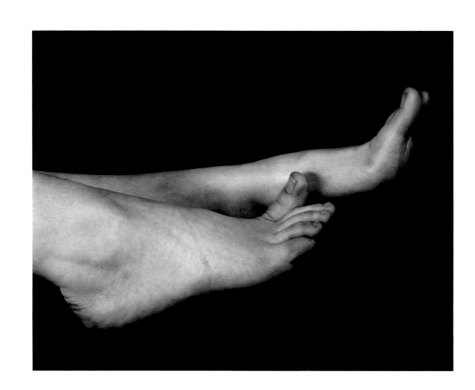

1934Edward Weston

1932 EDWARD WESTON

1933 EDWARD WESTON

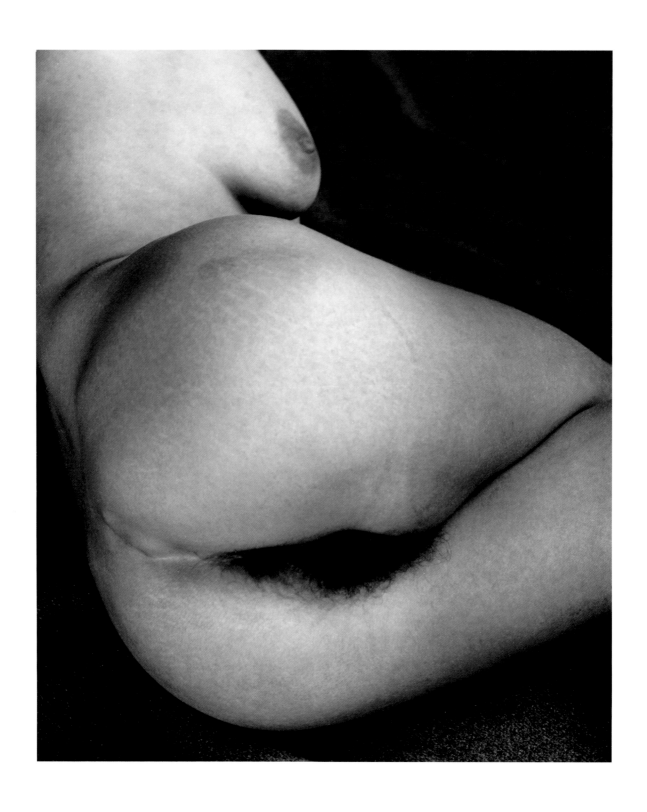

1933 EDWARD WESTON

1931 EDWARD WESTON

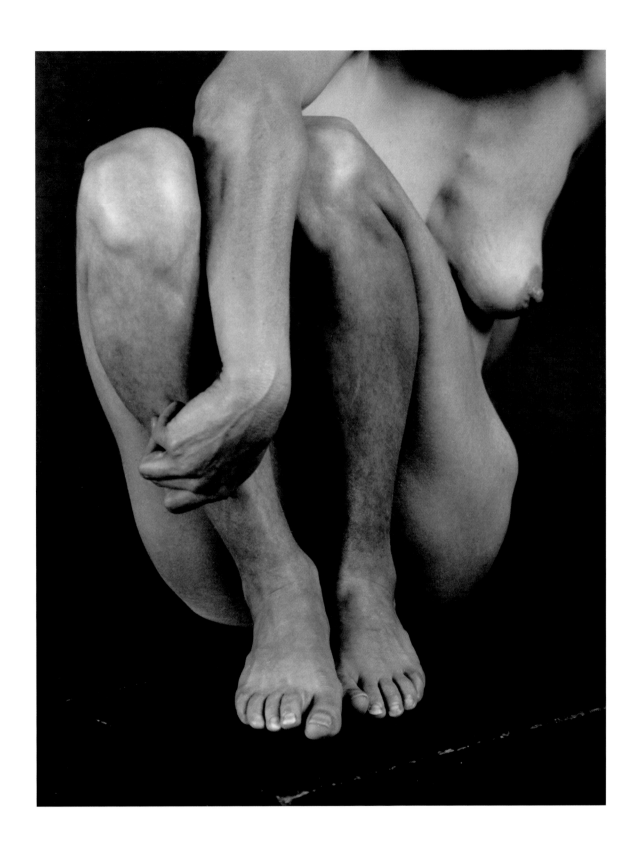

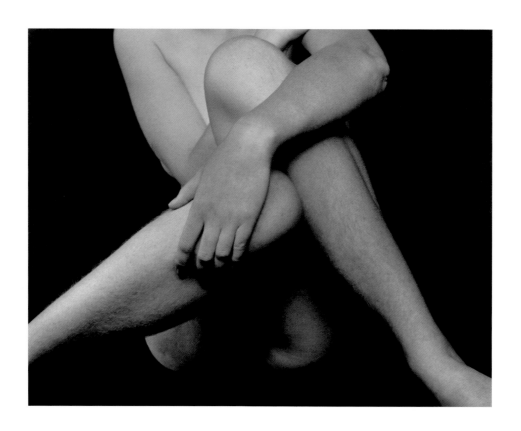

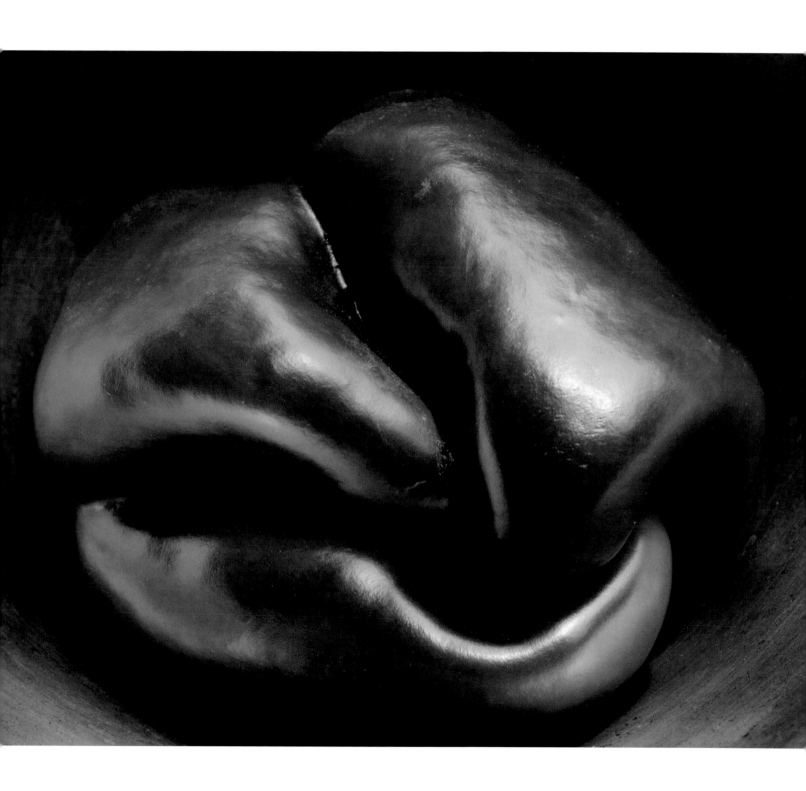

1929 EDWARD WESTON

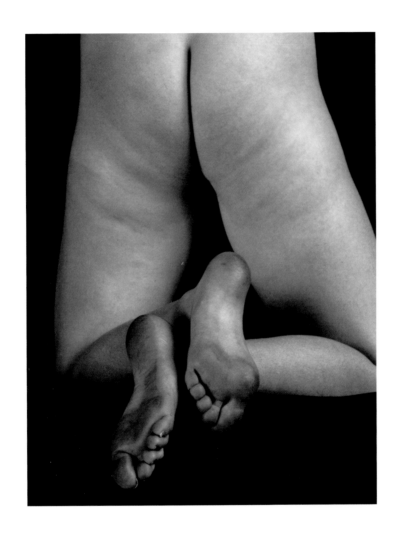

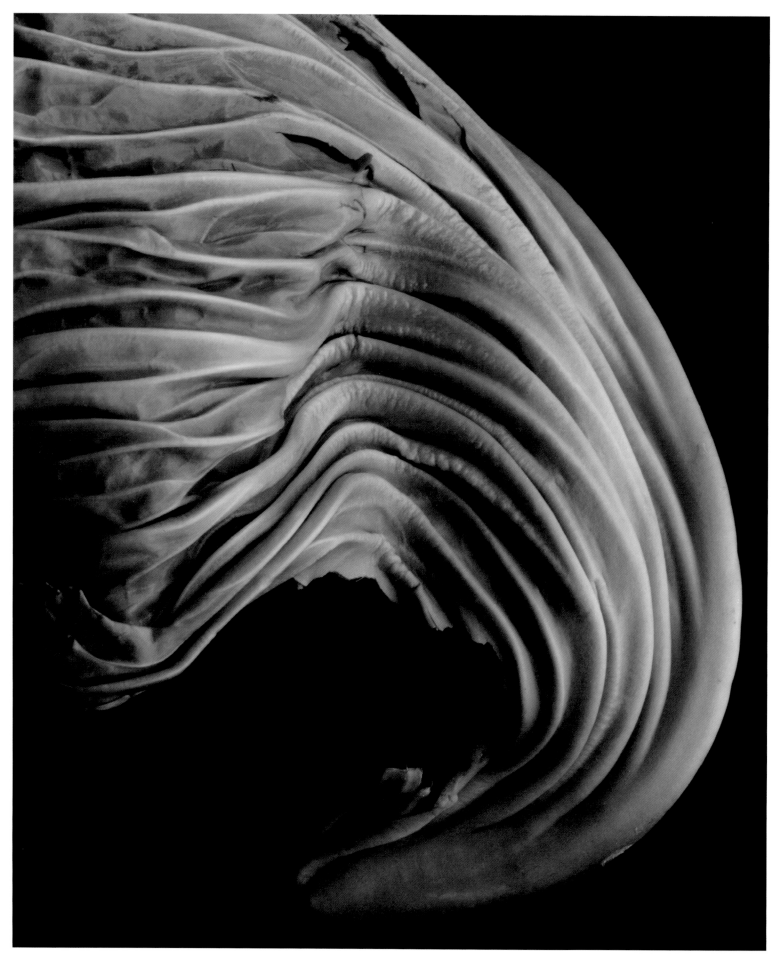

1931 EDWARD WESTON

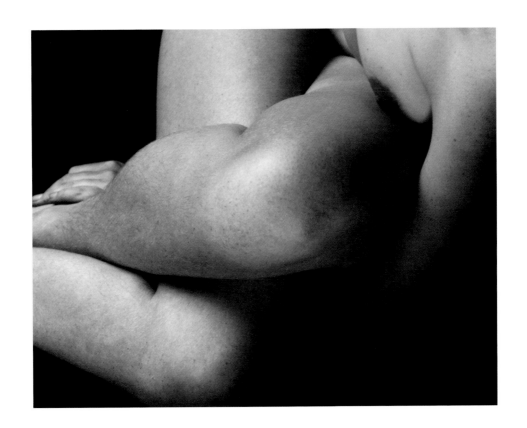

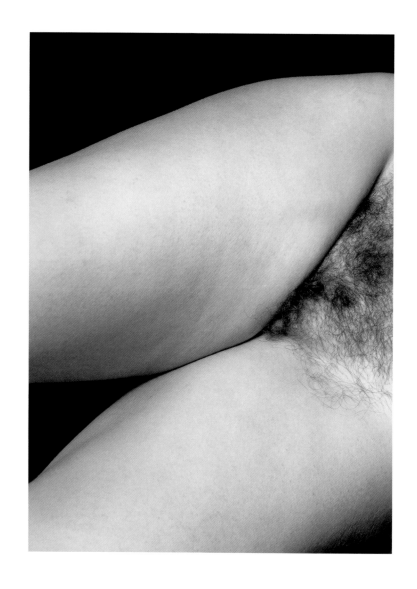

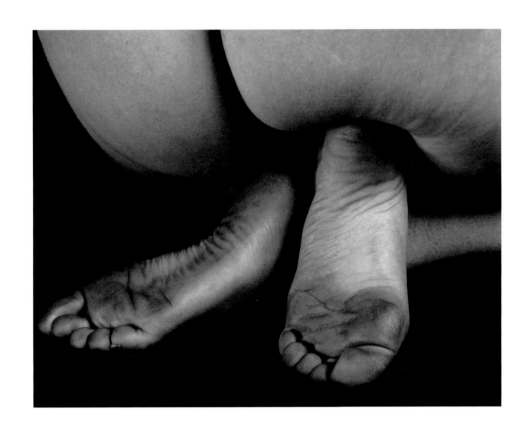

1954 Harry Callahan

1976H A R R Y C A L L A H A N

1936 EDWARD WESTON

1938Edward Weston

1927 EDWARD WESTON

1935 EDWARD WESTON

1927 EDWARD WESTON

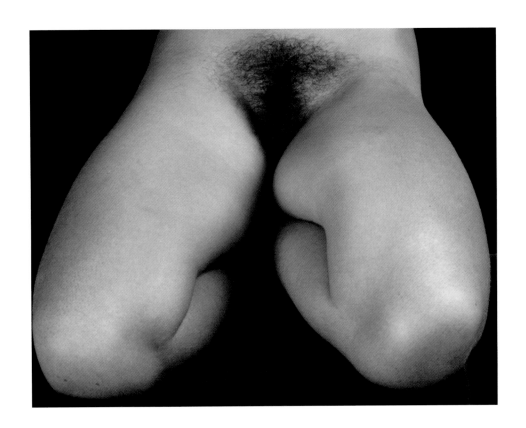

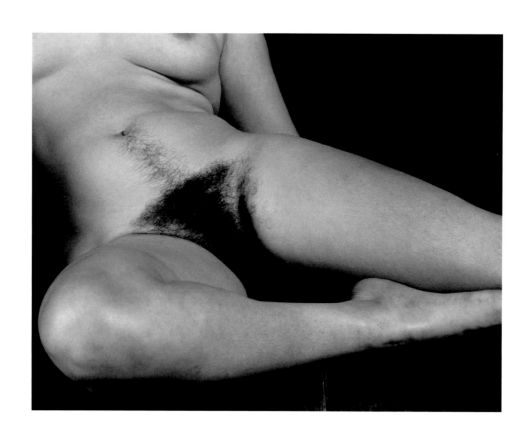

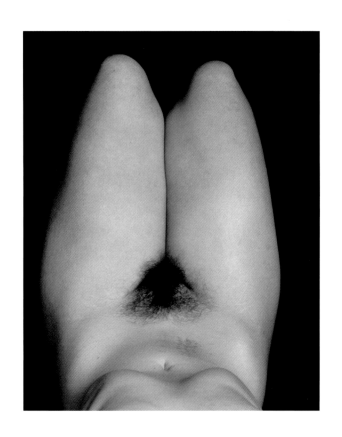

Edward Weston

Collection Center for Creative Photography, The University of Arizona
© 1981 Center for Creative Photography, Arizona Board of Regents

Harry Callahan

Collection Center for Creative Photography, The University of Arizona
Courtesy Pace/MacGill Gallery, New York
© The Estate of Harry Callahan

documents

WESTON | CALLAHAN

HARRY CALLAHAN. *WEEDS IN SNOW,*
negative and positive, 1943

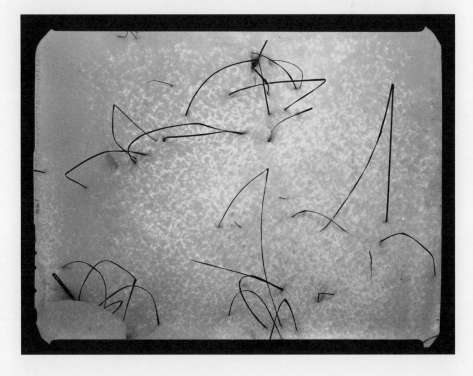

HARRY CALLAHAN. *ELEONOR NEGATIVES,* 1949

PAGES WITH THE VISITORS SIGNATURES FROM THE EXHIBITION OF EDWARD WESTON IN MÉXICO. Scrapbook of the author

MINOR WHITE. "THE PHOTOGRAPHS OF HARRY CALLAHAN". A review of the exhibit held at George Eastman House during January and February, 1958. Aperture, February 6th, 1958

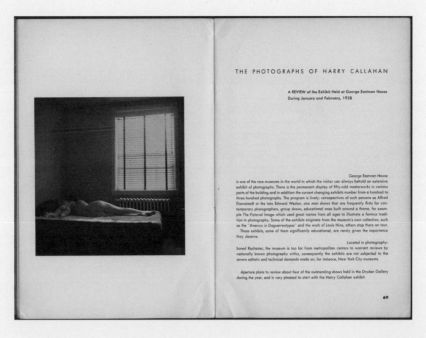

HARRY CALLAHAN. "AN ADVENTURE IN PHOTOGRAPHY", *MINICAM PHOTOGRAPHY,* February 1946

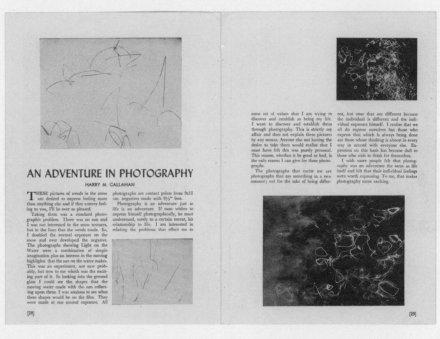

BERTHA WARDELL. LETTER TO EDWARD WESTON,
(ca. 1927)

I know you as a person of taste. As such you prize for
their sexual beauties – the delicacy of pearls, the glow of
rubies, the cool green water of esmeralds. That you are a
connoisseur only heightens the value of your judgment

Do you know the fingers of the wind on your body? We
must know together.
I shall think of you when I lie in the sun on the fine
white sand of the dunes this summer.

When I return–
If you still wish

EDWARD WESTON. EXTRACT FROM HIS DIARY,
March 24th, 1927

I have given my self a birthday present, it may be for a day, a year or forever, –I have quit smoking. This plan only happened to come on my birthday,– I have long considered to stop.

Bertha sat to me again: six negatives exposed,: all of some value, three outstanding, but two of the latter slightly moved.

However the one technically good is the one best seen. As she sat with the legs bent under, I saw the repeated curve of thigh and calf,– the slim bone, knee and thigh lines forming shapes not unlike great sea shells, the calf curved accros the upper leg, the shell's opening.

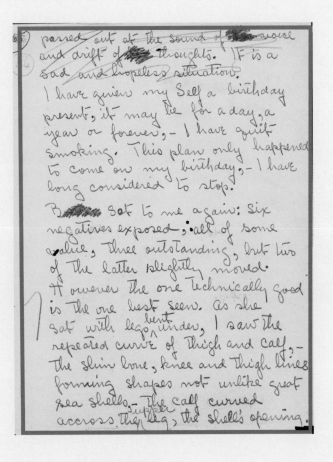

(FOLLOWING), March 24th, 1927

I made this, cutting at waist and above ankle.
After the sitting I fell asleep, sitting bolt upright,
supposealy showing Bertha some drawings,– I was that
worn out.

These simplified forms I search for in the nude body
are not easy to find, nor record when I do find them.
There is that element of chance in the body assuming
and important movement: then there is the difficulty in
focusing close up with a sixteen inch lens: and finally
the possibility of the movement in an exposure of from
20 sec. to 2 min.,– even the breathing will spoil a line.

If I had a work-room such as the one in S. Francisco
with a great overhead and side light, equal to out of
doors, I would use my Graflex: for there I made 1/10
exposures with f11. In this way I recorded Neil's body.
Perhaps the next nudes I will try using the Graflex
on tripod: the 8 inch Zeiss will be easier to focus,
exposures will be shorters, films will be cheaper!

My after exhaustion is partly due to the eye-strain
and nerve strain. I do not weary so when doing still-life
and can take my own sweet time.

B has a sensitive body and responsive mind. I would
keep on working with her.

EDWARD WESTON. EXTRACT FROM HIS DIARY,
March 30th and April 1st, 1927

The shells I photographed were so marvellous one could not do other than something of interest. What I did may be only a beginnig –but I like ~~two~~ one negative especially. I took a proof of the legs recently done of Bertha, which Miss Shore was enthusiastic over.

April 1st.
Nudes of ~~Bertha~~ again made but two negatives, –variation on one conception.

I am stimulated to work with the nude body, because of the infinite combinations of lines which are presented with every move.

And now after seeing ~~H Shore~~ the shells of Henrietta Shore, a new field has been presented. "I whish you would not do so many nudes, –you are getting used to them– the subject no longer <u>amazes you</u>, ~~some~~ most of these are just nudes". (I knew she did not mean they were just naked, but <u>that I had</u> lost my "amazement".)

Maybe if I had not shown her the whole series, but one or two selected ones, which is all I would ever finish from a series of Graflex negatives, her rection might have been different.

"You see Henrietta, I cannot possibly conceive my complete final result in advance, as you can. I hold to a definite <u>attitude</u> of <u>approach</u>, but the cameras can only record [what is in front of her, and so I must wait to be able to catch the right psychological moment"].

EDWARD WESTON. EXTRACT FROM HIS DIARY,
August 25th, 1927

August 25
I have been training my camera on a cantalope, –a sculptural thing. I know I shall make some good negatives for I feel it's form deeply. Then last eve green peppers in the market stopped me: they were amazing in every sense of the word– the three purchased. But a tragedy took place. Brett ate two of them!

Well I am joyful over my green pepper negative. If I can get some quality into the background it will rank with my finest expression. The cantalope is worthy of printing too, but I shall do it again, and of course I am not through with peppers.

Aug. 29 No –I am not through with peppers: now I have another as fine or finer, –the same pepper from another angle. Saturday I first made the first exposure: it was moved!– not badly, but enough to destroy that precision in my work which I want. I tried to say to myself it would do, but no, I can't fool myself.

EDWARD WESTON. EXTRACT FROM HIS DIARY,
February 21st, 1929

...That important asset of photography. In comparison there is my negative of the Juniper tree detail: it has exciting rhythms plus exquisite detail which no painter could record, –or if attempted must appear niggling, while in the photograph– an exact transcript of Nature and therefore exactly true– it is honest, convincing.

I also printed a nude, which in contrast makes the cliffs pale: the latter visually tremendous as seen in reality, –the former transformed by my way of seeing and understanding into something greater. This nude is months old,– and of X.

She leaned over in her acrobatic way –which might be called artificial, but is not artificial to her– until her breasts touched her thighs, –her arms followed the movement toward the base, completing a form of architectural solidity and significance. My best work is more analogous to architecture and sculpture than to painting. I made a posterior view, in flat but very brilliant light which outlines the figure with such a definite black line, that even photographers swear I have pencilled the negative, –I have used this light before on dancing nudes. The figure is presented quite symmetrically, great buttocks swell from the black centre, the vulva, which is so clearly defined that I can never exhibit the print publicly– the lay mind would misunderstand.

EDWARD WESTON. EXTRACT FROM HIS DIARY,
March 8th, 1929

Saturday 3-8–
Yesterday I made photographie history: for I have every reason and belief that two negatives of kelp done in the morning will someday be sought as examples of my finest expression and understanding. Another is almost as good, and yet another might be considered a very strong example of a more usual viewpoint: This latter several steps beyond the salon typ of photograph. But my two best, –they are years beyond.

I had found the kelp the ~~night~~ evening before, almost at the foot of the Ocean Avenue, washed there by the recent storm, the heavy sea. I knew it would not stay put, perhaps not even the night, so early next morning I walked down to see what the tides had done: and there it lay unchanged, twisted, tangled, interwoven, a chaos of convulsed rhythms, from which I selected a square foot, organized the apparently complex maze, and presented it, ~~as~~ a powerful ~~and organized whole~~ integration. This was done of course with no manual arrangement, –the selection was entirely my viewpoint as seen through the camera–.

I get a greater joy from finding things in Nature, already composed, than I do from my finest personal arrangements. After all, selection is another way of arranging: to move the camera an eight of an inch is quite as subtle as moving likewise a pepper.

EDWARD WESTON. EXTRACT FROM HIS DIARY,
April 24ᵗʰ, 1929

April 24 –I sent the following statement to Houston, Texas, where I am showing forty prints during May.

Clouds, torsos, shells, peppers, trees, rocks, smokestacks, are but interdependent, interrelated parts of a whole, which is Life. Life rhythms felt in no matter what, become symbols of the whole.

The creative force in man recognizes, and records these rhythms with the medium most suitable to him, to the object, or the moment, feeling the cause, the life within the outer form. Recording unfelt facts by acquired rule, results in sterile inventory. To see the Thing Itself is essential: the quintessence revealed direct without the fog of impressionism, the casual noting of a superficial phase, or transitory mood.

This then: to photograph a rock, have it look like a rock, but be more than a rock.

Significant presentation, –not interpretation.

EDWARD WESTON. EXTRACT FROM HIS DIARY,
August 8ᵗʰ, 1930

It is classic, completely satisfying, –a pepper– , but more than a pepper: abstract, in that it is completely outside subject matter. It has no psychological attributes, no human emotions are aroused: this new pepper takes one beyond the world we know in the concious mind.

Understanding, a mystic revelament, this is the «significant presentation» that I mean, the presentation through ones intuitive self, seeing, «through ones eyes, not with them: the visionary.

My recent work more than ever indicates my future.

HARRY CALLAHAN. LIST OF 4 X 5" NEGATIVES

F 422	ELEANOR SILHOUETTE		X
423	TREES WISCONSIN		
424	MULT. EL. WINDOW- BUSH		X
425	REEDS DET. 41		X
426	EL. PUBIC HAIR		
427	WEEDS IN SNOW		X
428	— —		X
429	— —		X
429 B	— —		X
430	WEEDS AIX		X
431	NIGHT SHOT CHI.		X
432	LEAF ON ICE DET.		X
433	ELEANOR FANNY		X
434	TREES AIX		X
435	GRASSES RI.		X
436	— PORT HURON		X
437	COBWEB AIX		X
438	— —		X
439	TREES —		X
440	WEEDS AIX		X
441	TREES —	SZARK	X
442	GRASSES		X
443	MULT EL. EGG		X
444	— DET. MAN		X
445	— ALLEY CHI.		X
446	— —		X
447	DAVISON SERIES		X
448	MUL EL. MOMA		X
449	DETROIT		
RF 1	CATTAIL SERIES		X
2	HUGO WEED		X
3	DET. —		X
4	EL. BREAST		X
5	— WATER		X
6	— DUNE		X
7	BUSH SNOW		X
8	PARK WATER BLOCK		X
9	EL. PREGNANT		X
10	— —		X
11	GRASSES BEACH EDGE		X
12	BARBARA HEAD		X
13	BUSHES IN SNOW		X

EL = (ELEANOR); DET = (DETROIT); SZARK = (JOHN
SZARKOWSKI); AIX = (AIX IN PROVENCE); RI= (RHODE ISLAND);
MULT = (MULTIPLE EXPOSURE); CHI = (CHICAGO)

FROM THE DAY BOOK OF EDWARD WESTON, 1931

Edited by B.N.

My work is always a few jumps ahead of what I say about it! I am simply a means to an end; I cannot, at the time, say why I record a thing in a certain way, nor why I record it at all! Why, indeed, does one give up material comfort for the sake of an idea, for "art"? Certainly public applause no longer spurs me on, though I want it, need it. The artist must fulfill his place as a giver. But maybe I am not an "artist," nor my product an "art"!

This question, an old and hackneyed one, was brought up again by a group of "real artists" (painters, of course) while viewing my recent retrospective exhibition. I set about at once to prove, by logical deduction, that photography could be an art—at least an art in the very terms these painters think in—and I proved it to my own satisfaction, though I am sure my logic would not even dent their defense mechanism. Then suddenly I realized I did not care what photography was labelled, that what I was doing had so much more importance and vitality than their painting that a great gulf separated their intent and mine.

This I have known for years. Most painters, and the photographers who imitate them, are "expressing themselves": "art" is considered as "self-expression". I am no longer trying to "express myself", or impose my own personality on nature. What I record is not an interpretation—my idea of what nature should be—but a revelation, a piercing of the smoke-screen artificially cast over life. Art is weakened according to the amount of personality expressed—to be explicit, according to the warping and twisting of knowledge by inhibitions. The artist is an instrument through which inarticulate mankind speaks: he may be a prophet who at a needed time points the way, or he may be born at a time when his work is a culmination, a flowering in soil already prepared.

So when, a few years ago, I wrote that I was no longer interested in interpretation, but in presentation, I was stating a half-truth. For after all,

EDWARD WESTON. EXTRACT FROM HIS
DIARY, EDITED BY NANCY NEWHALL,
1931

EDWARD WESTON

and the NUDE

The Nude is a basic human fact. We are all born naked! But that fact immediately clashes with another fact: for thousands of years we have not wandered unclothed about the earth, or if we did, were promptly clothed by scandalized neighbors or thrust briskly into jail. So we in turn clothe this cloistered phenomenon, the Nude, in illusions. When we meet with it in actuality, it astounds us - not by its beauty, which most of the time only the eyes of affection or the artist can detetct, but by its variations from our ideal.

But for equal thousands of years, artists have kept returning to the Nude because it is fundamental and vital. It is a reality - and a reality difficult to present in a world where it is rare and illogical. So the painters and sculptors have worn thin the few logical glimpses of intimacy, such as bathing and dressing, and they have worn out the Greek myths and the Bible. They have covered walls with Hercules and ceilings with Venus, and churches with everything from Adam and Eve to Susannah and the Elders. They have used the Nude as a symbol juxtaposed with other symbols; they have mined in the subterranean vistas of Freud.

To throw all this frippery out of the window takes the courage of a master. To present naked reality nakedly, you have to be a reality yourself.

The artist confronted by the Nude is as naked psychologically as his model in actuality. The painter's sleight-of-hand can no more conceal behind a convenient flutter of drapery who he is, at what stage of growth, and where his imagination halts, than the photographer can hide behind his camera, which has always revealed who is behind

**NANCY NEWHALL. "EDWARD WESTON
AND THE NUDE",** 1952

2

it more mercilessly than who is in front.

But the painter has free choice. He can ignore a vein, a mole, a fold of flesh - or accentuate them, as he pleases. He can omit a face, and change the broken, swollen feet of the porfessional model. The photographer must face every fact about his subject. If he cannot think how to turn an ugly fact inside out, he must sink it in shadow or leave it outside his groundglass. He has, however, one powerful ally - literally, the speed of light. He does not need the model who can fit back into a pose as if into a mould and simulate action by a careful equilibrium. Even with a big camera and slow exposures, he can come closer to the mecurial substance of humanity. With a small camera, or in bright light, he does not need posing; he can watch a living form in spontaneous motion, and seize instantly the significant moments.

To the painter, such moments (caught through photographs by himself or somebody else) are genesis; to him, reality is imperfect; it is the point from which he takes off. But the invention of photography gave another kind of men, formerly also painters, a medium closer to their desire. To photographers, reality is infinite. It is endless in its revelations to man. From galaxy to atom, from death to life, it is miraculous and exquisite. The chaos and the ugliness are only human blindness/ and stupidity.
The photographer's job is to understand and to reveal.

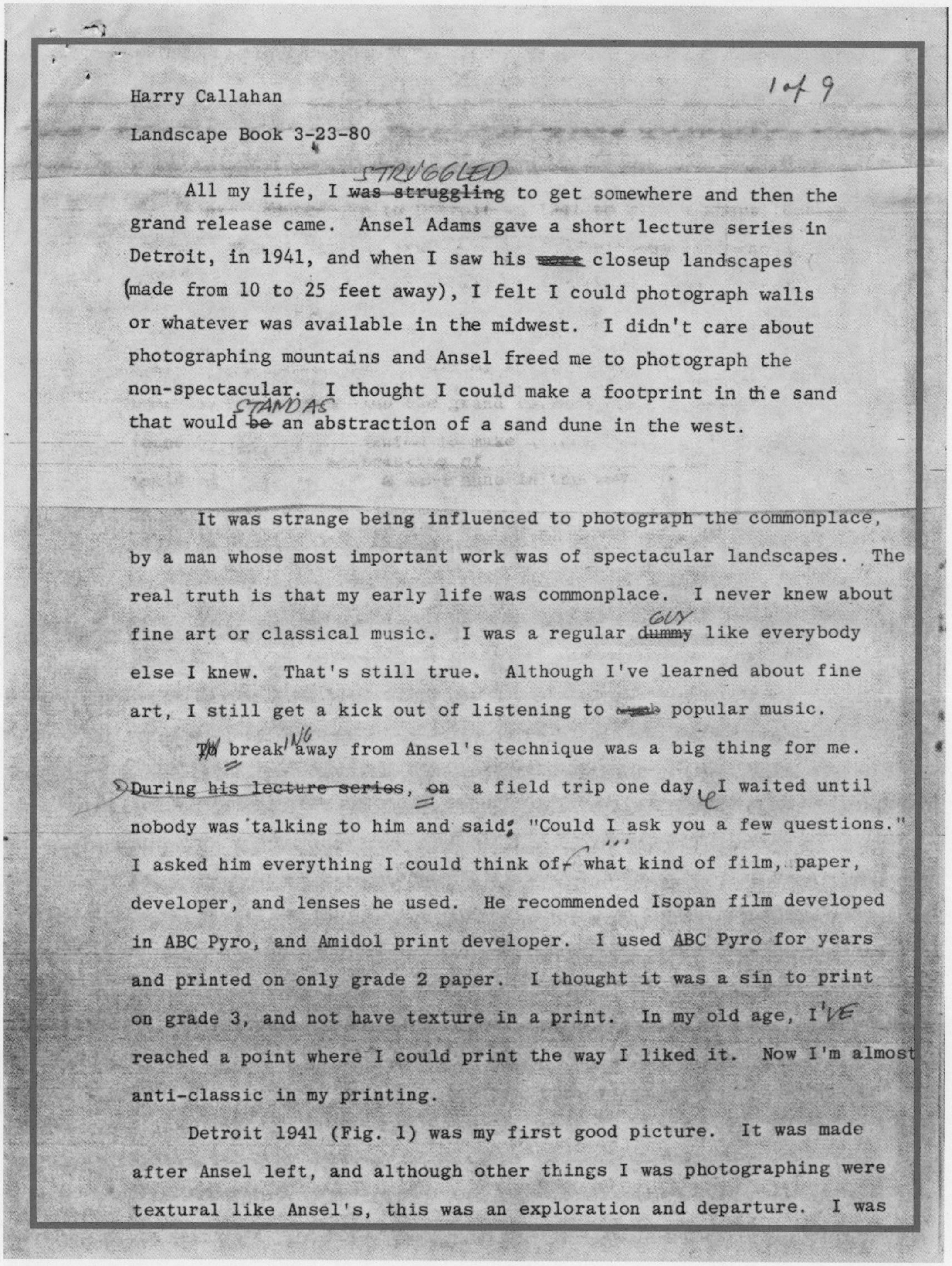

Harry Callahan

Landscape Book 3-23-80

STRUGGLED

All my life, I ~~was struggling~~ to get somewhere and then the grand release came. Ansel Adams gave a short lecture series in Detroit, in 1941, and when I saw his ~~were~~ closeup landscapes (made from 10 to 25 feet away), I felt I could photograph walls or whatever was available in the midwest. I didn't care about photographing mountains and Ansel freed me to photograph the non-spectacular. I thought I could make a footprint in the sand

STAND AS

that would ~~be~~ an abstraction of a sand dune in the west.

It was strange being influenced to photograph the commonplace, by a man whose most important work was of spectacular landscapes. The real truth is that my early life was commonplace. I never knew about

GUY

fine art or classical music. I was a regular ~~dummy~~ like everybody else I knew. That's still true. Although I've learned about fine art, I still get a kick out of listening to ~~~~ popular music.

NO

~~To~~ break away from Ansel's technique was a big thing for me. During ~~his lecture series,~~ ~~on~~ a field trip one day, I waited until nobody was talking to him and said; "Could I ask you a few questions." I asked him everything I could think of, what kind of film, paper, developer, and lenses he used. He recommended Isopan film developed in ABC Pyro, and Amidol print developer. I used ABC Pyro for years and printed on only grade 2 paper. I thought it was a sin to print on grade 3, and not have texture in a print. In my old age, I'VE reached a point where I could print the way I liked it. Now I'm almost anti-classic in my printing.

Detroit 1941 (Fig. 1) was my first good picture. It was made after Ansel left, and although other things I was photographing were textural like Ansel's, this was an exploration and departure. I was

HARRY CALLAHAN, *LANDSCAPE BOOK,*
March 23rd, 1980

June 26, 1931. Kootz - for book.

Talking, writing, - theorizing about one's work, assuming a credo, binds
one in a mental strait-jacket, difficult to escape. Dogmatic belief dams
the source of fresh impulse, dries up creative imagination, which can function
only when life is fluid and open to amazement over new discoveries. Growth
must not be halted for a day;

Growth, progress, change comes in the actuality of work, - in doing, not
talking. Intuition is the source of all creative work, - cold analysis
follows to explain, to deduce theories. But can there be an explantion?
If rationalizing could give reasons, not only would art be suffocated, there
would be no object in creating. For art begins where words end.

Having such a simple, flexible philosophy, I need not cannot, elaborate
further. I can write down how I have grown, what I have learned, from my
work in photography, my experience in life, see and felt, - discovered
through a lens, and considered in the quiet of a dark-room.

I have come to realize life as a coherent whole, and myself as a part, with
rocks, trees, bones, cabbages, smokestacks, all interelated, interdependent,-
each a symbol of the whole. And further, - details of these parts have their
own integrity, and through them the whole is indicated, so that a pebble x
becomes a mountain, a twig is seen as a tree.

Years of search through a camera, with it's precise, uncompromising single
eye, which sees more than our eyes are used to seeing, has made me conscious
of things in themselves, to present them directly without fanciful interpretation of transitory aspects, nor the subterfuge of manipulated, un-
photographic prints.

Recording the objective, the physical facts of things, does no preclude a
communication in the finished work of the primal subjective motive. An
abstract idea can be conveyed through exact reproduction, so that a cabbage
becomes more than a cabbage, - photography can be used as a means.

To use this penetrating, decisive camera vision, one cannot allow personal
psychology, pathological conditions to enter in: belly-aches or heart-
aches cloud the issue. Work, - do not rely on extraneous titillation. The
tempo of current life does not wait upon moods.

Photography meets the accelerated demands of today, - ready to record
instantaneously, shutter co-ordinating with vision at the cognizant
second of intensest impulse, one's recognition of life, or if need be, to
expose, to penetrate for hours into the very essence of the thing before the
lens.

My way of working in photography, my approach, given the discovery which
excites to focus, is this: I rediscover through my lens, - and a great
adventure it is! When the final form of presentation is seen, decided
upon the ground-glass, it is the finished print I prevision, complete in
every detail, in values and proportion. The shutter's release fixes for
all time this image, this conception, never to be changed by afterthought,
by subsequent manipulation. Significance must be realized before exposure.
The ultimate end, the print, is but a duplication of all that I saw, felt,
and brought to focus at that vital moment before exposure.

The foregoing definitely affirms my conviction in the importance of
"straight" photography. The photographer is quite as free to create within
the limits of his medium as the painter is within his limits: but the
painter cannot photograph with paint and brush, nor the photographer paint
with a camera. Creating is done with a force which guides the hand or
directs the camera: without wisdom, hand or camera are equally mechanical.
Leonardo da Vinci complained that musicians had placed painting among the
mechanical arts because it was done with the hand.

Authentic photography has it's own approach and technique. So understood
the medium is adequate, and unique in it's it's possibilities: but false
or perverted viewpoint - imitation -can only result in silly, mongrel
abominations.

Photography has revolutionized contemporary vision.   Edward Weston

EDWARD WESTON. "WRITINGS" STATEMENT FOR UNPUBLISHED BOOK,
June 26th, 1931

**DAVID ALFARO SIQUEIROS. "A PHOTOGRAPHIC
EFFORT OF CONSEQUENCE. THE WESTON-MODOTTI
EXHIBITION"**
El Informador, Guadalajara, September 4th, 1925

A PHOTOGRAPHIC EFFORT OF CONSEQUENCE
THE WESTON-MODOTTI EXHIBITION

The highest praise one can lavish on the photographic work of Mr. and Ms. Weston-Modotti, world-famous photographers whose choicest creations are now on display for the people of Guadalajara to enjoy in a hall at the State Museum, is that it constitutes THE MOST PURE PHOTOGRAPHIC EXPRESSION; indeed, the Weston-Modotti corpus is the most technically formidable example of what can be done and what MUST be done with the camera obscura.

The immense majority of photographers (I am thinking particularly of those who style themselves «serious photographers», «art photographers») squander the elements, the physical factors innate to photography itself, losing themselves in the quest for «pictorial» abstruseness; they assume that photography can take the same road as painting, and they spend their time producing forgeries of the early Italians, of decadent portraitists, of aristocratic women of Europe, of Impressionist painters, of the worst painters of these last fifty years.

Weston and Modotti, employing the same elements– or perhaps fewer elements, photographically speaking– which the bulk of photographers use to lie, to deceive others and themselves, by means of «artistic» TRICKS, make TRUE PHOTOGRAPHIC BEAUTY. The material qualities of the things and objects they portray could not be more APT: roughness is rough, smoothness is smooth, flesh is living, stone is hard. Things have a specific proportion and weight and are placed at a precisely defined distance from each other. In the sensation of REALITY imparted to spectators by the works of these two great masters, one must search for the PLEASURE, the BEAUTY, THE PHOTOGRAPHIC AESTHETIC, which differs from the PICTORIAL AESTHETIC not only by virtue of its very nature but also because it is diametrically opposed to the latter. One of photography's most salient merits is found in the organic perfection of details, a merit which, with the exception of the painters of the most abominable period in the history of painting –the academic period– did not concern any painter of the good schools that have existed. In a word, the BEAUTY encapsulated in the work of these photographers is simply– and herein lies its true worth –PHOTOGRAPHIC BEAUTY: a beauty that is absolutely modern and destined to take a surprising direction in the future.

The photographers Weston and Modotti know perfectly well, and so they prove in their works, that the only possible point of convergence between good photography and good painting (a point to which those «artists» who strive to make paintings with photography are entirely oblivious) is that in both good photography and good painting there must be a BALANCE, a RHYTHM of dimensions, of directions, of weights. And IN a specific proportion: the same whether the support is a wall to be decorated or a plate onto which a photograph is to be stamped. This is the reason why, in the works of these masters, a cluster of factory chimney stacks, a group of box houses, the position and angle of a woman's torso are always a source of profound beauty.

I firmly believe that an understanding and observation of industrial photography –that which aims to present a product in as perfectly and explanatory a way as possible, so as to excite the interest of the public, particularly the admirable industrial photography of machinery– served the photographers Weston and Modotti well, in that it allowed them to find the right road to photography as an AUTONOMOUS GRAPHIC EXPRESSION and therefore one of INTRINSIC BEAUTY; a road which they have naturally enriched with all the complementary factors it was lacking and which were indispensable to simple industrial photography.

Intellectuals, painters, photography experts and, in general, all men of intelligence and lovers of beautiful things, have at this moment a splendid opportunity to admire, in a hall at the State Museum, what may well be the work of greatest consequence in contemporary photography today.

ALFARO SIQUEIROS

Guadalajara, September 1925

El Informador - Guadalajara - Jal.
Sept. 14 - 1925

UNA TRASCENDENTAL LABOR FOTOGRAFICA

LA EXPOSICION WESTON-MODOTTI

El mejor elogio que se puede hacer de la obra fotográfica de los Señores Weston-Modotti, fotógrafos de fama mundial que actualmente exponen al Público de Guadalajara lo más escogido de sus producciones, en una sala del Museo del Estado, es que constituye LA MAS PURA EXPRESION FOTOGRAFICA; en efecto, la obra Weston-Modotti es la manifestación técnicamente más formidable de lo que se puede hacer y de lo que se DEBE hacer con la cámara obscura.

La inmensa mayoría de los fotógrafos (quiero referirme particularmente a los que se hacen llamar "fotógrafos serios", "fotógrafos artistas") desperdiciando los elementos, los factores físicos innatos a la fotografía misma, se pierden en rebuscamientos de carácter "pictórico"; suponen que la fotografía puede seguir los mismos caminos de la pintura y se dedican a confeccionar falsificaciones de primitivos Italianos, de retratistas decadentes, de mujeres aristocráticas de Europa, de pintores impresionistas, de pintores malos de estos últimos cincuenta años.

Weston y Modotti, con los mismos elementos —o quizá con menos elementos, fotográficamente hablando— que los que utilizan la mayor parte de los fotógrafos, para mentir, para engañar— a los demás y a sí mismos— por medio de TRUCOS "artísticos", hacen VERDADERA BELLEZA FOTOGRAFICA. Las calidades materiales de las cosas y de los objetos que retratan no pueden ser más JUSTAS: lo áspero es áspero; lo terso, terso; la carne, viviente; la piedra, dura. Las cosas tienen una proporción y un peso determinados y están situadas entre sí a una distancia claramente definida. En la sensación de REALIDAD que imponen al espectador las obras de estos dos grandes maestros hay que buscar el GUSTO, la BELLEZA, LA ESTETICA FOTOGRAFICA, que no solamente es diferente por su naturaleza misma de la ESTETICA PICTORICA, sino que es diametralmente opuesta. Uno de los valores importantes de la fotografía reside en la perfección orgánica de los detalles, valor que, exceptuando a los pintores de la más detestable época de la historia de la pintura: la época académica, no preocupó a ningún pintor de las buenas escuelas que hayan existido. En una palabra, la BELLEZA que encierran las obras de los fotógrafos que nos ocupan es simplemente —y en esto estriba su gran valor— BELLEZA FOTOGRAFICA; belleza ésta absolutamente moderna y que está destinada a tener en lo futuro un desarrollo sorprendente.

Los fotógrafos Weston-Modotti saben perfectamente bien, y así lo demuestran en sus obras, que el único contacto posible que puede haber entre la buena fotografía y la buena pintura (contacto que desconocen los "artistas" que quieren hacer pintura con la fotografía) es que tanto en la buena fotografía como en la buena pintura debe existir un EQUILIBRIO, un RITMO de dimensiones, de direcciones, de pesos, DENTRO de una proporción determinada; lo mismo tratándose de un muro que se tiene que decorar que de la placa sobre la cual se va a estampar una fotografía. Esta es la razón por la cual en las obras de estos Maestros, un grupo de chimeneas de una fábrica, un conjunto de cubos de casas, la colocación e inclinación del torso de una mujer, son siempre causa de profunda belleza.

Creo firmemente que la comprensión y la observación de la fotografía industrial —que tiene por objeto excitar ante el público lo más perfecta y explicativamente posible una mercancía, particularmente la admirable fotografía industrial de maquinarias—sirvió a los fotógrafos Weston y Modotti para encontrar el justo camino de la fotografía como MANIFESTACION GRAFICA AUTONOMA y por lo tanto de BELLEZA PROPIA; camino que naturalmente ellos han enriquecido con todos los factores complementarios que le hacían falta y que le eran indispensables a la simple fotografía industrial.

Los intelectuales, los pintores, los técnicos de la fotografía, y en general todos los hombres inteligentes y amigos de las cosas bellas, tienen en estos momentos la magnífica oportunidad de admirar en una sala del Museo del Estado, la obra quizá más trascendental de la fotografía contemporánea.

ALFARO SIQUEIROS.

Guad. Sept. 1925.

L.A. Times

PHOTOGRAPHY---AN EIGHTH ART?

*Reprinted From its June Issue by Courtesy of "The Argus"
of San Francisco This Article by a Great Camera
Artist Illuminates Photographic Art*

BY EDWARD WESTON

"A feeling for things in themselves is much more important than a sense of the pictorial," said no less an artist than Vincent Van Gogh.

Photographers the world over take notice! This great painter could have been writing for the majority of photographers, those, I mean, who are trying to express themselves through photography. If any medium is capable of rendering "things in themselves," it is photography. If any medium is misunderstood and abused it is photography.

In the foreword to the catalogue of a recent salon of pictorial photography I read, " . . . photography . . . a facile medium of artistic expression." A facile medium of artistic expression! Could any statement be more indicative of the weak approach to a medium of great potentialities? And the prints exhibited in this saloon revealed, in truth, a very facile attitude. Sometimes they were clever; often they showed technical skill in imitating paintings; seldom were they profound.

For contrast, read an important painter's estimate of photography:

"In these photographs the texture, the physical quality of things is rendered with the utmost exactness; the rough is rough, the smooth is smooth, flesh is alive, stone is hard. The things have a definite proportion and weight and are placed at a clearly defined distance, one from the other. In a word, the beauty which these photographs possess is photographic beauty." These words were set down by Alfaro Siqueiros of Mexico in 1925.

The great manufacturers have made photography so simple that I can teach a child of 10 to mechanically develop and print within a week's time. But that does not mean the ability to convey one's feelings so forcefully to another that they are likewise moved. To see the image on the ground glass as the finished print and to carry that image through all stages to an important conclusion is an ability achieved only after years of perseverance in acquiring the technique.

As to one's mental attitude, it must be quite the same as that of the worker in any other medium. One does not make of photography a holiday hobby and at the same time create in that medium. More than twenty years ago my father sent me a little kodak. My future was prefixed then, but only within the last few years have I been able to approach my problem with technical and mental surety.

Many fall by the wayside; others are content to dabble and indulge in mutual back-scratching; a few succeed in overcoming the difficulties, breaking through the mechanical barriers which might seem to exclude the camera as a means of personal expression.

In view of the difficulties to overcome the use of photography for any purpose other than commercial records can be justified only if it has advantages not to be had in any other medium.

And here the photographer who interferes with the purity of photography by manipulating his negative or print flounders and fails. He is blind to the beauty in an honest photograph—he must be an artist—and he produces arty results.

The lens reveals more than the eye sees. Then why not use this potentiality to advantage? To be sure, it is a dangerous power, and the tyro or weakling becomes confused, hiding his inability in a blur. The most delicate textures, the most evanescent forms, can be rendered by photography in an unbroken continuity impossible to the human hand. Fleeting expressions, salient gestures, passing phenomena can be captured forever.

I will even say—and not in defense—that it is immaterial whether or no these advantages have anything to do with art. Certainly they give photography undeniable value.

And since it has the vitality of a new expression, without traditions or conventions, the freshness of an experimental epoch, the strength of pioneering, photography has a significant status in the life of today.

The edition of these documents has been possible thanks to the collaboration between
PHotoEspaña and the Center for Creative Photography, The University of Arizona.